Dance, Lc
Ecstasy

The Modern Cult of Dionysos-Bacchus

JOHN KRUSE

GREEN MAGIC

Green Magic
53 Brooks Road
Street
Somerset
BA16 0PP
England

www.greenmagicpublishing.com

Designed and typeset by Carrigboy, Wells, UK
www.carrigboy.co.uk

ISBN 9781739973360

GREEN MAGIC

Contents

PART TWO. DIONYSOS IN MODERN CULTURE

Acknowledgments

Thanks are due to numerous individuals who provided the materials for this book. The websites theoi.com, topostext.org and attalus.org especially must be thanked for their labours in providing translations of the Greek and Roman texts that form the core of Part One. Many other individuals, who assembled ancient texts, poems, novels and works of art online should also be anonymously recognised for their services.

Extra special thanks go to the archives team at Trent University Library, Peterborough Ontario, as well as to the ever-helpful staff of the City of London Libraries and the British Library.

Introduction

> "I cried for madder music and for stronger wine,
> But when the feast is finished and the lamps expire,
> Then falls thy shadow, Cynara! the night is thine;
> And I am desolate and sick of an old passion,
> Yea, hungry for the lips of my desire:
> I have been faithful to thee, Cynara! in my fashion."[1]

Dionysos is the Greek god of the grape-harvest and winemaking, of the growth and fertility of vegetation – especially orchards and vineyards – and, lastly, of insanity, ritual madness, religious ecstasy, festivity and theatre. Because of his links to plant growth, he also became associated with death, resurrection and regeneration. He was also known as *Bákkhos* to the Greeks, a name adopted by the Romans as Bacchus.

My focus in this book will be on the links between Dionysos' cult and the perennial human preoccupations of drugs, sex and ecstasy.

1 Ernest Dowson, *Non sum qualis eram bonae sub regno Cynarae.*

On Ecstasy

The divine is always extraordinary and, for many religions around the world and throughout human history, overwhelming experiences that alter or expand a person's consciousness have been seen as an essential part of their faith and ceremonies. Whether these experiences come about because of a person's natural predisposition (as with some mystics), whether it's through techniques, such as meditation or movement, or whether the tool is drugs, the lucky individual is rendered capable of sensing something that others cannot, of contacting higher beings. Before the advent of the Dionysian cult in Greece, such experiences weren't unknown, but they weren't a central part of Greek religious practice either. Amongst the small number of native ecstatic cults, there were some worshippers of Artemis, Hecate, Pan and – notably – Cybele, whose *korybantes* celebrated the goddess with dancing and drumming.[2]

The aforementioned cults were of minor significance, but that of Dionysos attracted large numbers of adherents and it was especially concerned with frenzy and ecstasy. The latter word derives, through French and Latin, from the classical Greek *ekstasis*, from the verb *existanai* to put out of place – hence the phrase *existanai phrenon* 'to drive a person out of his wits.' The classical senses of *ekstasis* were 'insanity' and 'bewilderment' – the person had 'stepped outside' their everyday habits and patterns of thought; they lost their normal understanding and became subject to a mania or frenzy. However, in late Greek the etymological meaning received another application, that is, the 'withdrawal of the soul from the body, a mystic or prophetic trance.'

2 W. Burkert, *Greek Religion*, 1985, 109.

There are several means by which humans can experience ecstasy. They can ingest or inhale intoxicants, such as alcohol or opium fumes, or they can achieve the state by more directly physical routes – through meditation, dance or, of course, sex. The cult of Dionysos involved a combination of all of these to achieve its heightened consciousness or frenzied excitement.

In addition, the followers of the god were 'enthusiasts' – that is, in Greek *enthousiastes*: a person who is possessed or inspired by a god. In later Greek, *enthusiasm* denoted frenzy or inspiration; *entheos* meant that the god was within them. This merging of god and worshipper at ceremonies, a process that involved a public loss of self, are fundamental to the Dionysian cult, as shall be stressed repeatedly as the book proceeds.

PART ONE

Dionysos in the Ancient World

Names

The god Dionysos has been known by a remarkable variety of names and epithets across the ages and across cultures. To earlier generations, these were as familiar as they were to the ancient Greeks, so that many of these names may be encountered (unexplained) in poetry from the nineteenth and twentieth centuries. The following section therefore can act as a glossary for many of the poems that will later be mentioned as well as providing an overview of the many functions and guises of the god.

ETYMOLOGY

The first part of the god's personal name has been derived – since antiquity – from the genitive (possessive) form of the name Zeus – which is Dios. The second element – *nūsos* – is of uncertain origin, however; it may be associated with Mount Nysa, the birthplace of the god in Greek mythology, it may be connected to trees or it may mean 'son,' so that Dionysos is simply to be understood as meaning the 'son of Zeus' or, perhaps, 'young Zeus.'

Dionysos is also known as Bacchus (*Bákkhos*), the name adopted for the deity by the Romans; the frenzy he induces is *bakkheia*. It seems that the root of this name is the word *bakkhii,* which denotes the delirium brought about by drinking wine. Dionysos therefore became the god of the bacchantes, those frenzied by drink, rather than his followers being named after him. Whatever the precise derivations, these related words all serve to underline the identity between the god and his worshippers that existed at the core of the faith. An initiate to the god's mysteries became a *bakkhos* or *bakkhe* him or herself – a vital point to which we shall return frequently.[3]

3 M.A. Santamaria, 'Bakkhos,' in Bernabe, *Redefining Dionysos*, 2013, 38.

Another name used by the Romans was the Latin title *Liber,* which means 'free.' This was applied to the deity because of his association with wine drinking, and with the Bacchanalia and other rites, and hence with the freedom that was associated with these. His staff, called the *thyrsos*, which is sometimes wound with ivy and dripping with honey, is both a beneficent wand and a weapon used to destroy those who oppose his cult and the freedoms he represents.

The Roman name *Liber* is linked to another Greek label. As *Eleutherios* (the liberator), the god's wine, music and ecstatic dance freed his followers from self-conscious fear and care, and subverted the oppressive restraints of the powerful. As we've already seen, those who partake of his mysteries are believed to become possessed and empowered by the god himself. Lastly, the name Adoneus, which is both rare and archaic in Roman literature, is a Latinised form of Adonis. It was used as an epithet for Bacchus.

EPITHETS

> "The Boeotian Bacchantes called on Bacchus by his many noble names… [by] all the countless titles that are yours, Dionysos, throughout the lands of Greece."[4]

Dionysos was called *polymorphos* or *polyeides,* the many formed one, as well as "the serpent of a thousand heads" and "the god of a thousand names." He amply deserved these titles. He has been said to elude definition and to have ambivalent and paradoxical relationships to other deities. He is a god of vegetation, but was also envisaged as a dismembered child; he was a good of growth and life who at the same time had links with the world of the dead.[5]

4 Ovid, *Metamorphoses*, 4, 14.
5 W. Burkert, *Greek Religion*, 1985, 222.

The Greek historian Diodorus Siculus rightly recorded that "Many epithets, so we are informed, have been given him by men, who have found the occasions from which they arose in the practices and customs which have become associated with him." Down the ages and across the ancient world, Dionysos was, indeed, known by a vast variety of nicknames and additional or by-names. Fortunately, we can break these multiple titles down into several categories for better analysis.

Some of the names can appear in several categories because there are multiple potential explanations of their origins. The legends of Dionysos' early life are numerous and gave rise to many titles- although it is equally as likely that some of the legends were formulated to try to explain names whose true origins had been lost. There are also many names related to shrines found at particular places- these have not been listed.[6]

Sex & Love

Androgynos (androgynous in intercourse) – a title referring to the god's habit of taking both an active ('male') role and passive ('female') role during sex;

Arsenothelys – androgynous;

Choiropsalas – 'pig-plucker': from the Greek for pig, which was used as a slang term for the female genitalia. This is a reference to Dionysos' role as a fertility deity;

Dusales – hybrid;

Erikipeos – the androgynous one;

Gynnis – girlish;

Intonsus, the unshorn, alluding to the eternal (beardless) youth of the god;

Laphystios – the glutton;

Orthos – erect or rampant;

6 Diodorus Siculus, *Historia Biblioteca*, 4.5.1.

Phallen/phales – related to the phallus. At Methymna on Lesbos a famous wooden image of the god was dredged from the sea in some fishermen's nets. A local priestess declared it to look most like Dionysos *Phallen*, to whom a shrine was duly established;[7]

Pseudanor – literally 'false man' or 'falsely virile,' referring to the divinity's feminine qualities; and,

Psilas – the unbearded.

Wine

Especially notable is the fact that Dionysos/Bacchus is the god of wine and the bringer of joy and oblivion. Many of his names are associated with this – but the blood-like look of wine might also link with his functions as a resurrected deity.

Acratophorus – giver of unmixed wine;

Agathus Daemon – the good spirit;

Braetes – a term related to brewing beer;

Hygiates – health-giver, because of the psychological benefits of moderate drinking in company;

Iatros – delight;

Lenaius – god of the wine-press or vats;

Lyaeus, or *Lyaios* – 'deliverer,' literally 'loosener,' one who releases from care and anxiety;

Lysius – delivering, releasing from guilt;

Mainomenos – the drunken god;

Melpomenos – god of joyful songs; named after the dramatic muse;

Morychus – 'smeared,' because his icon was smeared with wine lees at the vintage.

Oeneus – wine-dark, denoting Bacchus as the god of the wine press;

Omphakites – the god of the unripe grape;

7 Pausanias, *Description of Greece*, 10, 19, 3.

Polygethes – bringer of joy; *charma brotoisin,* the god of many joys, is clearly related;
Protrygaios – the first of the vintage;
Psilax – on uplifted wings. The reason for this name is that "wine uplifts men and lightens their spirit no less than wings do birds;"[8]
Skyllitas – related to the vine-branch;
Staphylites or *staphylos* – the god of the grape, whence *poly-staphylos,* he of the abundant clusters, is also derived; and,
Theoinus – wine-god of a festival in Attica.

Lordship

Aisymnetes or *aesymnetes* – the one who is lord or who rules;
Agrionos – savage;
Agyieus – protector of ways; also used in reference to pillars or altars dedicated to the god that were set up in the streets;
Anthroporraistes – man-destroyer;
Briseus – he who prevails;
Enyalios – the warlike;
Eubouleus – the god of good counsel;
Indoletes – meaning slayer of Indians- due to Dionysos' legendary campaign against the people of India;
Meilichios – the god that can be propitiated, or the gracious;
Melanaigis – armed or clad with a black aegis;
Patroios – paternal;
Pergetes – the benefactor;
Sisopolis – city saviour; and,
Thesmophoros – law-giver.

Resurrection

Bromios – roaring, as of the wind or thunder; this primarily relates to the central death and resurrection element of the

8 Pausanias, *Description of Greece*, 3, 19, 6.

god's myth, but also to the god's transformations into lion and bull and the boisterous sounds of those who drink alcohol;

Chthonios – the subterranean one;

Erechtheos – conceived in the underworld;

Erikryptos – completely hidden;

Morychos – the dark one;

Ploutos – wealth, but also related to Pluto/ Hades;

Taurophagus – meaning bull eating and *tauros* – a bull. This beast is linked to Dionysos' myth of rebirth after his murder by the Titans. He is also called *tauromorphos* (bull-shaped). Sophocles recorded that in Athens an ox was given to the god by the winners of the dithyrambic (poetry) competition held at the annual festival of Dionysia. The name *bougenes,* calf, may also be related.

Nature & Fertility

Aegobolus – the goat-shooter or killer. This appears to relate to the goat's reputation as a natural enemy of vines, but may also refer to offerings of goats' blood to the vines;

Agrios or *Agrionios* meaning wild;

Anthion or *antheros* – of the flowers;

Auxites – giver of increase;

Dendrites – he of the trees. Dionysos was patron of all cultivated trees. He helped them grow and presided especially over orchards;

Endendros – the one in the tree. In fact, the earliest representations of the god were simple wooden posts, perhaps draped with a cloak and with a mask for a face;

Enorches – with or in the testicles. This relates to reproduction but also to one of the myths of Dionysos' birth (see later);

Hyes – the moist or fertilising god;

Iraphiotes/eriphos – goat-kid. The god sometimes took the form of a goat. It was said that when Zeus' wife Hera took against the baby Dionysos and plotted his death, his father turned him into a goat to conceal him from her. At festivals he was often symbolised by serving a goat kid stuffed with apples, which were a symbol of immortality. There was a festival to Dionysos in Attica called *Phellos* – apparently after the word *phellea,* which denoted a rocky area of grazing suitable for goats;

Isodaites – the god who distributes his gifts/sacrifice equally to all;

Kemilius – young deer;

Kissos – god of ivy;

Liknites – he of the winnowing fan or harvest basket. The baby deity was placed in a fan as a cradle and, too, may have sailed across the ocean to Greece seated in it;

Melanaigis – of the black goatskin. If he didn't appear as a goat (see *iraphiotes* above), Dionysos might appear wearing a goatskin as a sign of his affinity;

Mielekos – sweet, like honey or figs;

Pelekys – god of the axe;

Perikionius – climbing the column – i.e. ivy, a plant perennially associated with the god;

Phleon – the giver of plenty or luxurious foliage,

Phleus – an adjective related to the bloom of a plant;

Phytalmios – god of plant growth;

Semeleios – meaning 'he of the Earth', 'son of Semele,' and a reference to one of his birth stories;

Sykites – related to figs. Another name was *meilichios,* from *meilicha,* figs. The god was also called 'the well fruited,' 'he of green fruit' and the one who made fruit grow. Pomegranates are also linked to Dionysos, symbolising the blood that was shed when the Titans dismembered him as a child (see later);

Thyllophorus – bearing leaves; and,

Triptolemos – sower.

Cult

Aisymnetes – masked;

Bakcheutos – the loud one;

Bassareus a name that derives from the *bassaris* or fox-skin, as worn by celebrants of the mysteries. The *bassara* or *bassaris* was the long robe which the god himself wore;

Bougenes – borne by a cow, in the Mysteries of Lerna;

Epaphaios – inspiring frenzy;

Eriboas – the howler;

Evius – echoing cry;

Gynaimanes – inspirer of frenzied women;

Iacchos – lord of cries or shouts;

Katharsios – purifier;

Kistophorus – 'basket or ivy-bearer,' which alludes to baskets being sacred to the god;

Lampteros, the shining or torch-bearer. This name relates to the god's rites being performed at night in pine groves, lit by torches. At Pellene there was a sanctuary dedicated to this particular manifestation of the god; local people celebrated a festival called the *Lampteria* (the feast of torches), during which they brought burning brands into the sanctuary at night and set out bowls of wine throughout the entire city;[9]

Maenoles – mad or raging. This phrase is first found in the *Iliad* and relates to the orgiastic nature of the god's worship;[10]

Maenomenos – mind-expander, the leader of the maenads;

Melpomenos, the singer – see too *erikapaios,* the eternal singer;

Mystes – of the mysteries;

Nyktypolos – nocturnal;

Omadios/omestes – a flesh-eater, a name relating to human sacrifice to the god;

Perikionos – the pillar, because of the earliest manner of representing the god;

---

9 Pausanias, *Description of Greece*, 7, 27, 3.

10 Homer, *Iliad*, 6, 130.

Philopaigmos – friend of the satyrs;
Soter – meaning 'the saviour;'
Soterios – recovery from madness;
Thuoneus – the one who is raving or inspired (a term related to 'enthused');
Trieterikos – god of alternate festival years; and,
Zagreus – the horned or hunting god.

Life Story

Dimetor – twice-born. This may originally have related to viticulture, seeing the god as being born first in the sprouting plant and secondly in the swelling grapes. However, separate legends grew up to describe his two physical births, as we shall see later. *Amphietes,* god of two years, and *dissotokos,* the god of two origins, are doubtless related names, as may be *dimorphos* (see below), god of two shapes, although this may relate to his shapeshifting abilities. Robert Graves described this ability wonderfully, stating that Dionysos "perpetually changes… into an infinity of shapes… as a wild bull, as a many headed snake, or as a fire-breathing lion- whichever he pleases;"[11]

Dimorphos – Dionysos was known as the god of two forms because, suggested Diodorus Siculus, "there were two Dionysoi, the ancient one having a long beard, because all men in early times wore long beards, the younger one being youthful and effeminate. Certain writers say, however, that it was because men who become drunk get into two states, being either joyous or sullen, that the god has been called 'two-formed';"[12]

Dithyrambos – used at his festivals, referring to his premature and double births;

11 Graves, *White Goddess*, 1961, 134.
12 Diodorus Siculus, *Historia Biblioteca*, 4.5.2 & 4.5.3.

Ignigena (in Latin) or *pyrigenes* (in Greek) – born of fire. This may be related to the idea that toadstools are caused by lightning, which is hurled by Zeus (see later);
Kouros – boy;
Limnaios – marsh born;
Merotraphes – literally a seam-splitter, which probably relates to the god's legendary birth from Zeus' thigh – hence the god was also called *eiraphiot* (the 'in-sewn');
Nysian – according to legend he founded the city of Nysa;
Pentheus – this title is linked to the word meaning suffering or pain and it seems that part of the god's cult involved the idea that he faced and overcame obstacles and suffering;
Protogonos – first born;
Sphaleotas – the lame one. Robert Graves connected a lop-sided gait with eroticism because it might emphasise the buttocks. Apparently Greek prostitutes were called 'salmakides' because they wiggled their bottoms (*saleuma*);[13]
Telagios – of the sea;
Thriambus – this name was given because the god was the first who was recorded to have celebrated a triumph (*thriambos*) upon entering his native land after his campaign in India, whence he returned on an elephant with great booty;[14] and,
Trigonos – thrice born (see above).

Divine Nature

Aysios – the one who liberates;
Braites – the breaker;
Eleutherios (the liberator), this epithet was, interestingly, shared with Eros;

13 Graves, *White Goddess*, 325.
14 Diodorus Siculus, *Historia Biblioteca*, 4.3.1 & 4.5.2.

Hugiates – dispenser of health; the byname *iatpos* had the same meaning. At his famous oracle of Amphicleia in Phocis, Dionysos cured diseases by revealing their remedies through sufferers' dreams. The use of the name *theos soter* (saviour god) that was mentioned earlier related to his powers over disease as much as to his conquest of death and rebirth;[15]

Kechenos – brave;

Lampter – light;

Lysius – destroyer or deliverer;

Mitrephoros – wearer of a crown;

Musagetes – god of the muses;

Saotes – saviour.

Lastly, one Greek poet combined all the traits of Dionysos together into one paean of praise, addressing him as:

> "Jealous, very wrathful, envious, bestower of envy, gentle, sweet drinker, sweet-voiced, cozener, Thracian, thyrsos-bearing, boon-companion, lionhearted, slayer of Indians, desirable, twiner of violets, hierophant, reveller, horned, ivy-crowned, noisy, Lydian, lord of the wine-press, dispeller of care, healer of sorrow, mystic, frenzied, giver of wine, thousand-shaped, god of the night, shepherd-god, fawn-like, clothed in fawn-skin, Spear-thrower, common to all, giver of guests, yellow-haired, prone to anger, stout of heart, lover of the mountain shade, wanderer on the mountains, deep drinker, wanderer, wearer of many garlands, constant reveller, mind-breaker, slender, wrinkled, clad in sheep-skin, leaper, satyr, son of Semele, jovial, bull-faced, slayer of Tyrrhenians, swift to wrath, chaser of sleep, liquid, hymeneal, dweller in the woods, mad for wild beasts, terrible, laughter-loving, wanderer, golden-horned, graceful, relaxer of the mind, golden-filleted, disturber of the soul,

15 Pausanias, *Description of Greece*, 10, 33, 11.

> liar, bent on noise, tearer of the soul, seasonable, eater of raw flesh, nurtured on the mountains, making clamour on the mountains."[16]

Read all together, many of these labels and qualities suddenly seem contradictory and impossible to confine within a single person. Like so many deities, but particularly Dionysos, that is central to his nature. He is multi-faceted and complex and, because of this, he can offer to devotees a range of powers. He is a traditional god of fertility, from which developed his function as the patron of wine – and thence song, joy and drunkenness. Generalising further from the fact of inebriation, we can see Dionysos as a healing god, who releases worshippers from their anxieties. Elaborating further from this concept as a liberator, the deity was recognised as conqueror of mortality as well as the quotidian sufferings of daily life. Dionysos stands for ecstasy and relief and, as such, he was revered in ancient times and still fascinates us today.

16 *Greek Anthology* Book 9, 9.524

Dionysos – Life & Career

Dionysos was one of the earliest gods attested in mainland Greek culture. The first written records of his worship come from the palace of Nestor in Pylos, dating to around 1300 BCE. Even at this very early period, the offering or payment of wine seems to have been involved. Other records from Pylos record the worship of a god named Eleutheros, a figure who was also regarded as the son of Zeus, and to whom oxen were sacrificed. The links to both Zeus and oxen, as well as the semantic links that exist between the names of Eleutheros and the Latin deity Liber Pater, suggest that this god may simply have been Dionysos by another name.

Even at this early date, then, there were multiple forms of the god and/or confusion about his origins. This suggests in turn that the original roots of the Dionysian cult long predate historical sources and that the accounts of his life and feats had been passed on orally for many generations.

STORIES OF THE GOD & HIS COMPANIONS

By the seventh century BCE, Dionysos was already being worshipped as more than just a god of wine. He had come to be associated with weddings, death, sacrifice, and sexuality, and his retinue of satyrs and dancers was already firmly established. A common theme in many early stories and depictions of the god and his followers was the idea of metamorphosis: the god could change himself and those around him into other creatures. It seems that this is an early manifestation of the idea that his cult represented an opportunity for celebrants to escape – or to be liberated – at least temporarily – from the confines of their ordinary lives.

Dionysos was also sometimes celebrated as a bringer of order, law and peace, although it does have to be remarked that the god's often-violent progress through the world as a youth, his severe treatment of detractors, and the generally rowdy nature of his followers (not least after a few bowls of wine) all sit rather ill with this association.

A number of accounts and traditions existed in the ancient world regarding the parentage, birth, and life of Dionysos on earth, a picture that was further complicated by his several rebirths. By the first century BC, attempts had been made to harmonise the various accounts of Dionysos' birth into a single narrative which involved not only multiple births, but two or three distinct incarnations of the god on earth over several lifetimes. These in turn gave rise to the idea that there were younger and older forms of the god, the former being youthful and effeminate, the older bearded.

As has already been suggested, Dionysos was a shapeshifter. He was at times conceived of as a sacred child, but he might also appear as a range of animals and he might die, only to rise again. He could cast glamour on other people and items, for instance changing their outward form, changing water to wine or making them appear to be on fire.[17] Dionysos was the only Greek god who could grant life as well as deprive a person of it. He had many powers: he enjoyed the gifts of healing and prophecy, he bestowed fertility and he wielded magic. Certainly, Dionysos' links with prophecy tend to be forgotten or underplayed, but it should be recalled that he was the first oracle at Delphi, so that this attribute must be seen as fundamental to his nature. In the *Bacchae,* this aspect of his divine character is made explicit: "this god is a prophet – for Bacchic revelry and madness have in them much prophetic skill. Whenever the god enters a body in full force, he makes the frantic to foretell the future."[18]

17 Euripides, *Bacchae*, 620–25.
18 Euripides, *Bacchae*, 299–300.

BIRTH & CHILDHOOD

According to Robert Graves, Dionysos may originally have had no parents at all, instead being generated (like mushrooms) when a bolt of lightning sent by Zeus struck the fertile ground.[19] As this particular story demonstrates, one fact of Dionysos' birth is constant – and that is the involvement of Zeus in some way or other. As we learned in the previous chapter, this is only to be expected given that the young god's name seems explicitly to relate him to Zeus. In fact, in many aspects of his character and function, Zeus closely parallels or resembles his son: for example, he oversaw the growth of vines, sending ripening light and warmth, and one of his Roman festivals, *Vinalia*, marked the wine harvest – as its name indicates. These festivals were also dedicated to Venus, and involved offerings by 'common girls' and prostitutes at one of her shrines – an interesting combination of sex and wine in one event.

Later, though, Dionysos was granted both father *and* mother, from which point his birth stories started to multiply and elaborate. The thirtieth Orphic hymn to the god described him as "occultly born in beds ineffable," a deft summary of his complex and mysterious nativities.

Initially, Dionysos was believed to have been born from the coupling of Zeus, who had assumed snake-form, and Persephone, who was his own daughter and wife of Hades. Because his mother ruled as the queen of the underworld, Dionysos was seen as representing the 'chthonic' or underworld aspect of his father.

Another version of his birth makes Dionysos son of Demeter, goddess of agriculture (and mother of Persephone), a maternity that underlines his function as the god of growth and natural life. Historian Diodorus Siculus emphasised the symbolism of this particular account: Dionysos, god of the vine, was born from the union of the gods of the rain and the earth.

19 Graves, *White Goddess*, 159.

The fate of this first Dionysos was to be bodily torn apart and boiled by the giants called the Titans, who were the sons of Gaia, or Earth. They had seen the baby god seated upon Zeus' throne in his absence and they feared that he was destined to become Zeus' heir and ruler of the cosmos – a role that the Titans had once enjoyed before being displaced by the Olympians. They were encouraged in their plot by Zeus' wife Hera, who performed the archetypal role of wicked stepmother and was violently jealous of this child. After his death and dismemberment, the child's body was presented to Hera, who cooked and ate it. According again to Diodorus Siculus, this murder is symbolic of the harvesting and crushing of the grapes to make wine. Furthermore, just as the remains of the stripped vines were returned to the earth to restore its fertility, so in Diodorus' version the remains of the young Dionysos were returned to Demeter, allowing him to be born again.[20]

Many Greeks believed that Dionysos was born a second time, after his murder by the Titans. His second conception arose from the coupling of Zeus and the mortal woman Semele (whose name in fact means 'Earth' in Phrygian – hence Dionysos is again born of a union of sky and earth). One version of this second conception states that Zeus gave Semele the dismembered heart of the baby Dionysos in a drink and she was impregnated as a result. In another telling, Zeus once again took snake shape to couple with her. Immediately after this, Semele's bed and chambers were overgrown with vines and flowers, and the earth laughed. Zeus then informed her of his true identity and told her to be happy: "you shall bring forth a son who will never die, and you I will call immortal. Happy woman! you have conceived a son who will make mortals forget their troubles: you shall bring joy to both gods and men."[21] During her pregnancy, Semele rejoiced in the knowledge that her son would be divine. She dressed herself in

20 Diodorus, 3.62–74.
21 Nonnus, *Dionysiaca*, 7

garlands of flowers and wreathes of ivy, and would run barefoot to frolic in the meadows and woods whenever she heard music.

In one variant of the Semele story, she asked to see her lover in his true, divine form. Zeus appeared as a bolt of lightning, which struck and killed (the motif of lightning striking the soil and giving rise to the child again). Zeus saved his son, though, a sowed the baby up in his thigh until he could be born. This episode caused Victorian art critic Walter Pater to observe that, thereby, "the story of Dionysus has become a story of human persons, with human fortunes, and even more intimately human appeal to sympathy." The young god's losses made his story subtler, tempering it with sorrow- and enhancing its attraction for us.[22]

Most accounts say the baby god was born in Thrace. After this, according to the Greek poet Nonnus, Zeus gave the infant to Hermes to take care of him and he in turn entrusted the child to the river nymphs called the Lamides. This divine protection proved important, as the boy survived several further attempts upon his life by the jealous Hera until he reached adolescence. Another account of his childhood records that Dionysos was taken to be raised by the rain-nymphs of Nysa. In recognition of their devoted care for the child, Zeus rewarded the nymphs by placing them in the heavens as the Hyades star cluster.

Yet another version states that the baby was cared for by the nymph Mystis on the island of Euboea. She is the goddess nymph who oversaw the Bacchic mysteries – as her name indicates. Her son was Korymbos (ivy berries) and she is also sometimes called Makris or Kombe, mother of the korybantes or protectors of the infant god.

Sometimes, too, it is said that the child god was raised by the muses or by 'bassarids,' the word that is used to denote the women who participated in the ceremonies of the god Dionysos (see later). The twenty-sixth *Homeric Hymn to Dionysus* describes

22 Pater, *Greek Studies*, 1895, 24 & 43.

how, once the boy-god was old enough, he would wander the woods, a train of the "rich-haired nymphs" following him, thereby prefiguring his later retinue of bacchae. According to the Byzantine patriarch Photius, the growing boy in time became a pupil of the centaur Chiron, who taught him chants and dances, the bacchic rites and initiations.[23]

When Dionysos reached his teens, he made two important discoveries that were to be of lasting benefit to mankind. Firstly, he discovered how to cultivate vines and the method of extracting and fermenting the grapes' juice, being the first person ever to do this. Apparently, this happened by accident. Playing with the other children, he cut a fennel stalk and hit rocks with it, whereupon they broke and wine flowed out. Another account suggests that the vine was discovered on the slopes of Mount Olympus- very evidently a gift of the gods.[24]

The poet Nonnus of Panopolis dramatised the discovery of viticulture in his story of the god, the *Dionysiaca*, describing how, when human life recovered after the flood, it lacked revelry in the absence of wine. "Without Bacchus to inspire the dance, its grace was only half-complete and quite without profit; it charmed only the eyes of the company when the circling dancer moved in twists and turns with a tumult of footsteps, having only nods for words, hand for mouth, fingers for voice." Seeing this, Zeus had declared that he would send his son to teach mortals how to grow grapes and make wine, thereby alleviating their toil and suffering.[25]

Dionysos' second important discovery that he taught to people was the technique of ploughing with oxen. As a result of this, he was often shown with horns or was referred to by various bull epithets (which linked him with Egyptian Osiris). His names (as we have already seen) included bull-shaped, bull-faced, cow-horn, bull-horned, horn-bearing, horned, two horned and bull-

23 Nonnus, *Dionysiaca*, 14; Photius, *Bibliotheca*.
24 Oppian, *Cynegetica*, 4, 230.
25 Nonnus, *Dionysiaca* 7.

browed. His festival at Elis involved women calling upon him to come to the temple, "rushing with your bull's foot, oh goodly bull!" Bacchantes in Thrace would mark the same connection by wearing horns during their festivities.

Despite these juvenile triumphs, Hera finally exacted her vengeance upon the second Dionysos, striking the young man with madness and driving him away. His father Zeus had already predicted that the young Dionysos would struggle on earth, but that he would in due course be received "by the bright upper air to shine beside Zeus and to share the courses of the stars."[26] For a time, he was to become a wanderer over the earth, accompanied by his retinue of satyrs, Pans and warrior bacchae (these women are sometimes called nymph maenads to distinguish them from the god's later human followers). He carried with him animal skins full of wine and dispensed his knowledge of viticulture, but in a number of places he met with resistance and rejection of the gift of the vine, something to which he always reacted violently and vengefully. His harsh responses seem at odds with his reputation as jolly Bacchus and are hard to explain; perhaps they were a consequence to the undeserved enmity of Hera, which made him distrustful and insecure.

After spending some time in Greece and Asia Minor, Dionysos then set out on an expedition through India teaching the people the cultivation of the vine. He again met with resistance but, with his devoted host, he subdued opposition, founded cities and bestowed new gods and laws on the people. According to Diodorus Siculus, Dionysos in fact conquered the whole world except for Britain and Ethiopia. These campaigns were full of incident, all of which have contributed to the mythology and iconography of the god.

Finally, in Phrygia, the goddess Cybele (who was known to the Greeks as Rhea) purified Dionysos and cured him of his madness (although a second version says that it was a visit to

26 Nonnus, *Dionysiaca* 7.

his father Zeus' shrine at Dodona that provided the remedy). Very importantly for the future direction of his cult, Cybele then taught the young god her religious rites of initiation or mysteries (again, other accounts say that this knowledge came from the nymph Mystis or from Chiron).

The 'orgies' that Dionysos learned from Cybele involved the use of tambourines, drums, cymbals and castanets, pipes, dance and the singing of hymns. These rites took place outside at night, lit by torch-light. The goddess also supplied the young deity with his 'gear,' which must include not only the musical instruments just mentioned but the *thyrsos* staff we shall discuss later.

WINE

> "Medicinal, holy flower: mortals find in you repose from labour, delightful charm, desired by all mankind."[27]
>
> "Wine is a great comfort to a weary man..."[28]

Dionysos is the god of all aspects of viticulture and wine-making, including its sale by merchants and, inevitably, its enjoyment in company. As the reborn god, he personifies the vine, which is cut back in the autumn but produces new shoots and new fruit each year; in this respect, he represents the life-force of the cosmos.

Dionysos symbolises too the exhilaration brought about by drinking the fermented grape juice. The god's cult originated in Thrace, the inhabitants of which were notorious amongst the ancient Greeks for their frequent inebriation; his worship inherited from those roots its ecstatic character, involving wild dancing to exciting music – and drinking, plenty of drinking... However, the aim – it must be emphasised – was not merely to get legless. Wine frees you from your woes, but in the rites of Dionysos intoxication is much more about intensifying your mental powers than losing all your faculties.

27 *Orphic Hymn to Dionysos*, 50.

28 Homer, *Iliad*, 6.260.

The special relationship between the god and the vine may neatly be demonstrated by a story from Mount Larysion in Lacedaemon. This spot was sacred to Dionysos, and at the beginning of each spring the local people held a festival in his honour. It was said that his approval and gratitude for this mark of respect was shown by the fact that a ripe bunch of grapes would always appear at the site.[29]

Very similar was a tradition from Elis in southern Greece. The people of the city were said to have worshipped Dionysos with the greatest reverence, for which reason they believed that the god attended their festival, the *Thyia*. At the start of the *Thyia* three empty pots were placed by the priests inside the temple, the entrance of which would then be sealed. On the next day the doors would be opened and the pots would be found filled with wine, as a tangible (and potable) sign of the god's favour.[30]

Viticulture

The Greek poet Hesiod said that Dionysos gave mankind both grapes and fermentation vats. Euripides confirmed this, explaining that the god "gives to mortals the vine that puts an end to grief." Wine is, in fact, almost a sacrament: "Another [of the Bacchae] let her thyrsos strike the ground, and there the god sent forth a fountain of wine."[31]

Dionysos taught people the art of pruning the vines as well as making wine from the grapes. The Roman author now known to scholars as Pseudo-Hyginus expanded upon the curious manner in which this discovery came about:

> "The ancient men of our race had, on the posts of their dining-couches, heads of asses [Dionysos' sacred beast]

29 Pausanias, *Description of Greece*, 3, 22, 2.

30 Pausanias, *Description of Greece*, 6, 26, 1–2; Athenaeus, *Deipnosophistae*, 2, 34a.

31 Hesiod, *Works and Days*, 609 & *The Shield of Heracles*, 398; see also Pseudo-Hyginus, *Fabulae*, 129–130; Euripides, *Bacchae* 535, 650, 705 & 770.

> bound with vines to signify that the ass had discovered the sweetness of the vine. The vine, too, which a goat [another of Dionysos' sacred animals] had nibbled, brought forth more fruit, and from this they invented pruning."[32]

Dionysos used his divine powers to manipulate the climate and ensure a year-round supply of grapes. He also protected them from unwanted predators:

> "Dionysos has cunningly fixed the seasons of the vines so that he may gather a continuous harvest. The clusters are so abundant that they both hang from the rocks and are suspended over the sea, and birds of both the sea and the land fly up to pluck them; for Dionysos provides the vine for all birds alike except the owl, and this bird alone he drives away from the clusters because it gives man a prejudice against wine. For, if an infant child that has never tasted wine should eat the eggs of an owl, he hates wine all his life and would refuse to drink it and would be afraid of drunken men."[33]

As has already been observed, the god's own life could serve as a metaphor for wine production:

> "Dionysos was named twice-born (*dimetor*) by the ancients, counting it as a single and first birth when the plant is set in the ground and begins to grow, and as a second birth when it becomes laden with fruit and ripens its grape-clusters – the god thus being considered as having been born once from the earth and again from the vine."
>
> "There is a spring called Kissousa (of the ivy) [on Mt Kithairon]. Here, as the story goes, his nurses [the nymphs

32 Pseudo-Apollodorus, *Bibliotheca*, 2.191; Pseudo-Hyginus, *Astronomica* 2.2 & *Fabulae* 274.

33 Philostratus, *Imagines*, 2.17.7.

> of Mount Nysa] bathed the infant Dionysos after his birth, for the water has the colour and sparkle of wine, is clear, and is very pleasant to the taste."[34]

As we see, Dionysos became linked too with water-worship, with the worship of the spiritual forms of springs and streams (the nymphs). To summarise, as Walter Pater realised, Dionysos was the soul of vine and, thence, "the dispenser of the earth's hidden wealth."[35]

Drinking

The finished product was, of course, a source of joy and consolation. As one writer said of Dionysos, "He leads laughter (*gelos*) and revel (*comus*), two spirits most gay and most fond of the drinking-bout."[36]

Love, desire and – even – satisfaction (provided that over-indulgence has not intervened) are inextricably intertwined with wine. People lose their inhibitions and may say and do what they otherwise would not dare to:

> "[Dionysos] ... is great in other respects, and they say this too of him, as I hear, that he gives to mortals the vine that puts an end to grief. Without wine there is no longer Kypris [Aphrodite, as goddess joy and pleasure] or any other pleasant thing for men."[37]

Homer described some of the other effects of indulgence: "This is the effect of your wine- for wine is a crazy thing: it sets the wisest man singing and giggling like a girl; it lures him on to dance and it makes him blurt out what were better left unsaid." It might

34 Diodorus Siculus, *Library of History*, 3.62.5; Plutarch, *Life of Lysander*, 28.4.
35 Pater, *Greek Studies*, 1895, 13 & 27.
36 Philostratus, *Imagines*, 1.25.3.
37 Euripides, *Bacchae*, 770.

be proposed that another aspect of the idea of rebirth that's associated with the god is just this effect of wine. It can render people youthful again; it can encourage them to cast off the seriousness, respectability and propriety of age; it can even get mature males to reveal their girlish sides. It might be added that acting like a girl might perhaps be done in honour or imitation of the god (see later).[38]

As is of course well known – and is painfully learned – Dionysos' greatest gift is a mixed blessing to mankind. The ancient writers had a lot to say about wine – and much of that was either ambivalent or negative. That's because, whilst the boon of gaiety is matched by the diminution of cares, both of these can too easily turn into the regrets of oblivion and the hangover the next day:

> "The gods, in pity for the human race thus born to misery, have ordained the feasts of thanksgiving as periods of respite from their troubles; and they have granted them as companions in their feasts the muses, Apollo the master of music, and Dionysos."[39]
>
> "Bacchus delights in being mixed as the fourth with three nymphas [he's added to three parts water]; then he's most ready for the bedroom."

Whether the drinker wants to lie down to sleep – or something else – is left to our imaginations.

> "Let us be merry and drink wine and sing of Bacchus, the inventor of the choral dance, the lover of all songs, leading the same life as the *Erotes* (loves), the darling of *Kythere* [Aphrodite as goddess of pleasure]; thanks to him, drunkenness was brought forth, the grace was born, pain takes rest and trouble goes to sleep."[40]

38 Homer, *Odyssey*, 14.464.

39 Plato, *Laws* 653d.

40 *Euenus*, Fragment 2; *The Anacreontea*, Fragment 38

In his play *The Bacchae,* Euripides recorded a long statement of what must have been the contemporary Greek attitude to the inebriation. It was a balancing act with a splitting headache, admittedly, but its benefits could outweigh the physical cost:

> "[Wine] releases wretched mortals from grief, whenever they are filled with the stream of the vine, and gives them sleep, a means of forgetting their daily troubles, nor is there another cure for hardships. He who is a god is poured out in offerings to the gods, so that by his means men may have good things... [Dionysos] holds this office, to join in dances, to laugh with the flute, and to bring an end to cares, whenever the delight of the grape comes at the feasts of the gods, and in ivy-bearing banquets the goblet sheds sleep over men... To the blessed *and* to the less fortunate, he gives an equal pleasure from wine that banishes grief."[41]

Dionysos also became the god of truth in that people will say what they really think when they're drunk (although repentance of this too may come with the dawn):

> "Dilphios the comic poet says: 'O Dionysos, dearest and wisest in the eyes of men of sense, how kind art thou! You alone make the humble to feel proud, and persuade the scowler to laugh, the weak to be brave, the cowardly to be bold.'"[42]

Sometimes – if you're lucky perhaps – the drink deprives drinkers of the power of speech before they can say too much and make a fool of themselves: "Such gifts as Dionysos gave to men, a joy and a sorrow both. Whoever drinks to fullness, in him wine becomes violent and binds together his hands and feet, his tongue also and his wits with fetters unspeakable: and soft sleep embraces him."

41 *Bacchae*, 275–80, 375 & 420.

42 Athenaeus, *Deipnosophistae*, 2.35d.

Perhaps this is another, more subtle, gift of the god, protecting his devotees from themselves?[43]

Lastly, Euripides declared Dionysos "the most terrible [god] and yet most mild to men." Presumably the terrible aspect is the hangover – although the Greek rhetorician Athenaeus, of Naucratis reminded his readers that Dionysos also taught the art of mixing wine with water so that it wasn't so strong. The first man to be taught this skill was Amphictyon, who promptly set up altars to the phallic Dionysos and, curiously, to the Nymphs (see earlier).[44]

Author Diodorus Siculus also warned that the drinking of unmixed wine resulted in a state of madness, but that the effect of mixing it with the rain from Zeus was that delight and pleasure could be enjoyed without the ill effects of madness and stupor. The same writer also suggested that the god recommended the mixing of wine because some of his own followers got drunk and then hurt each other fighting. For the same reasons, the *thyrsos* was a hollow fennel stem: previously his retinue had carried staves, which had contributed to the injuries inflicted; the fennel stems would instead simply snap if used offensively.[45]

For all the public praise of Dionysos' gift, therefore, its costs were well known and moderation was recommended:

> "Mnesitheus [a Greek physician] said that the gods had revealed wine to mortals, to be the greatest blessing for those who use it aright, but for those who use it without measure, the reverse. For it gives food to them that take it, and strength in mind and body. In medicine it is most beneficial; it can be mixed with liquid drugs and it brings aid to the wounded. In daily intercourse, to those who mix and drink it moderately, it gives good cheer; but if you overstep

43 Hesiod, *Catalogues of Women*, Fragment 87 as cited in Athenaeus, *Deipnosophistae*, 10.428.

44 *Bacchae* 863; Athenaeus, *Deipnosophistae*, 2.38c-d.

45 Diodorus, 4.3.4, 4.4.6 & 4.4.7.

> the bounds, it brings violence. Mix it half and half, and you get madness; unmixed, bodily collapse. Wherefore Dionysos is everywhere called *Latros* (Physician)."[46]

In the so-called Orphic inscriptions, the god Euboulos ascribed the following wise advice to Dionysos:

> "Three bowls only do I mix for the temperate: one to health, which they empty first, the second to love and pleasure, the third to sleep. When this is drunk up, wise guests go home. The fourth bowl is ours no longer, but belongs to violence; the fifth to uproar; the sixth to drunken revel; the seventh to black eyes. The eight is the policeman's, the ninth belongs to biliousness, and the tenth to madness and hurling the furniture. Too much wine, poured into one little vessel, easily knocks the legs from under the drinkers."

Sensible self-regulation can be difficult, depending upon personality and situation, driving some, such as Plato, to conclude that only state intervention would work:

> "[In the ideal city] We shall rule that the young man under thirty may take wine in moderation, but that he must entirely abstain from intoxication and heavy drinking. But when a man has reached the age of forty, he may join in the convivial gatherings and invoke Dionysos, above all other gods, inviting his presence at the rite (which is also the recreation) of the elders, which he bestowed on mankind as a medicine potent against the crabbedness of old age, that thereby we men may renew our youth, and that, through forgetfulness of care, the temper of our souls may lose its hardness and become softer and more ductile, even as iron when it has been forged in the fire."[47]

---

46 Athenaeus, *Deipnosophistae*, 2.63a–b.
47 Plato, *Laws* 665b.

The associations between Dionysos, wine, poetry, pleasure – and regrets – persisted down the ensuing centuries. For example, John Milton described how it was "Bacchus, that first from out of the purple grape/Crushed the sweet poison of misused wine" and how the sorceress Circe fell for this "blithe youth" with his "clustering locks," their relationship resulting in the birth of a son Comus, whose name means 'revelling,' as we saw, and is probably linked with 'comedy.' This young deity and his companion Pan were the source of drama, but also of "riot and ill-managed merriment" and of "wanton dance" to the sound of pipes and flutes.[48]

ADULTHOOD

After his excursions and conquests in the east, Dionysos arrived back in Greece as a foreigner, even though the evidence we have already seen indicates that, in fact, he was one of Greece's oldest attested gods. His attribute of foreignness – as an arriving outsider god – may be inherent and essential to his cults, as he is a god of epiphany, of revelation and realisation, sometimes being called "the god that comes."[49]

Resistance & Sanctions

Returning in triumph to his home, Dionysos came to be considered the founder of the triumphal procession, a tradition that was adopted in time by Roman emperors. Far more importantly, he strove to introduce his religion into Greece, yet was opposed by rulers who feared it, on account of the disorder and madness amongst celebrants that it involved. The consequences of this scepticism and doubt were violence and retribution. A distinctive

48 Milton, *Comus*, 1638, lines 45–58 and 172–177.

49 See, for example, R. Taylor-Perry, *The God Who Comes: Dionysian Mysteries Revisited*, 2003.

aspect of the classical cult of the deity was the fact that he was known for wreaking punishment upon unbelievers, often by striking them with destructive madness that drove them to kill family members or mutilate themselves. Those who interfered with or obstructed the god's rites or mysteries, his *orgia,* were especially vulnerable to sanction.[50]

In one myth, adapted in Euripides' play *The Bacchae*, Dionysos returned to his birthplace, Thebes, which was under the rule of his cousin Pentheus. Pentheus, as well as his mother Agave and his aunts Ino and Autonoe, disbelieved Dionysos' claims to divine birth. Despite the warnings of the blind prophet Tiresias, they denied him any special status, refused to worship him and denounced him for inspiring the women of Thebes to madness. In response, Dionysos used his divine powers to drive Pentheus insane. He then encouraged him to spy on the ecstatic rituals of the maenads, in the woods of Mount Cithaeron. Pentheus, hoping to witness a sexual orgy between the women ("like birds they are in the bushes, held in the sweetest grips of love"), hid himself in a tree.[51] The maenads spotted him but, maddened by the god, they took the king to be a mountain-dwelling lion, and attacked him with their bare hands and tear him limb from limb. To add to the bitter irony of this vengeance, Pentheus' aunts and his mother Agave had been seized by the delirium and were among the maenads. Agave fixed her son's head on her thyrsos and took her trophy to her father Cadmus. Only then the madness passed, at which point Dionysos appeared in his true, divine form, banishing Agave and her sisters and transforming Cadmus and his wife into serpents.

A very similar story is told of King Lycurgus of Thrace. When he learned that Dionysos was in his kingdom, he imprisoned all the maenads. Dionysos fled but inflicted a drought on the land which provoked the people to revolt. The god next drove King

50 Diodorus Siculus, *Historia Biblioteca*, 4.3.4.
51 Euripides, *Bacchae*, 957.

Lycurgus insane, causing him to chop up his own son with an axe in the belief that he was a patch of ivy (a plant holy to Dionysos). An oracle then predicted that Thrace would remain dry and barren as long as Lycurgus was alive, so the population had him drawn and quartered. His anger assuaged by the king's fall and destruction, Dionysos lifted the curse he had placed on the kingdom. In an alternative version of this story, Lycurgus tried to kill Ambrosia, a follower of Dionysos, who was transformed into a vine that twined around the enraged king and slowly throttled him.[52]

Madness and loss of self-control therefore lie right at the heart of the Dionysian cult. The god's own youthful career was born of the madness inflicted by his envious mother-in-law, Hera, and trance-like ecstasy lay at the heart of his ceremonies, bringing his worshippers into personal communication with him. However, just as the exhilaration of drunkenness can get out of hand, the psychic delirium brought by Dionysos can have a dark as well as a beneficial side.

Other stories describe how Dionysos could neither be captured or confined by his enemies. In one tale, an attempt by Tyrhennian (Etruscan) pirates to kidnap him with a view to selling him into slavery ends with the men all being turned into dolphins by the god. As shown by this transformation of the pirates, Dionysos wields magical or divine powers that enable him to transform objects. An apt illustration of his abilities comes from the island of Andros. Philostratus described how a stream of wine appeared there, and the islanders became drunk, because "by act of Dionysos the earth of the Andrians is so charged with wine that it bursts forth and sends up for them a river; if you have water in mind, the quantity is not great, but if wine, it is a great river – yes, divine! [There] the men, crowned with ivy and bryony, are singing to their wives and children, some dancing on either bank, some reclining. And very likely this also is the theme

52 Homer, *Iliad*, 6.136–137.

of their song… this river makes men rich and powerful in the assembly, and helpful to their friends, and beautiful and, instead of short, four cubits [six feet] tall; for, when a man has drunk his fill of it, he can assemble all of these qualities and in his thought make them his own. They sing, I feel sure, that this river alone is not disturbed by the feet of cattle or of horses, but is a draught drawn from Dionysus, and is drunk unpolluted, flowing for men alone."[53]

Death & Rebirth

Dionysos' most significant adult adventure as his *katabasis*, or descent into the underworld. He entered into the afterlife in order to rescue his mother Semele, who was reputed to have died soon after his birth (or conception).

There were various obstacles and challenges to overcome, but eventually Dionysos and his mother emerged from the underworld through waters of a lagoon – thus symbolically being reborn after a period of time with the dead. He renamed his mother Thyone, and ascended with her to heaven, where she became a goddess.

Following this triumph, Dionysos' divine nature was finally acknowledged by all the gods and he too ascended to Olympus. His worship then began at shrines across Greece, most notably on Naxos. With these many temples were associated numerous festivals throughout the year, which attracted large crowds from across the Greek world. The events tended to feature drinking (naturally), processions, dramatic performances, dancing, games, sacrifices and choral singing. In some cases, the crowds were known to dance *en route* to the shrines as well. These festivals and ceremonies will be described in detail later.[54]

53 Philostratus, *Imagines*, 1.25.1 & 2.

54 Pausanias, *Description of Greece*, 10, 4, 3.

SEXUALITY

There is a strong gay or bisexual element to Dionysos' character. This even applies at his birth: in one account, he was born from the thigh of his father, Zeus, an image with clear erotic and even homoerotic connotations. Certainly, in later life he had several male lovers as well as plentiful female partners.

Gay Dionysos

Although the oldest images of Dionysos show a mature, full-bearded man, this was increasingly displaced by representations that depicted him as young, long haired and with soft, rounded features, almost effeminate. These are the two forms of the god mentioned previously. Walter Pater suggested that this change followed Dionysos' transition from rural to urban deity.[55]

One myth related to Dionysos' youth involves his love for the Thracian boy Ampelos, who was part-satyr:

> "It is said that the beardless Ampelos, son of a nymph and a satyr, was loved by Bacchus on the Ismarian hills. Upon him the god bestowed a vine that trailed from an elm's leafy boughs, and still the vine takes from the boy its name. While he rashly picked the ripe grapes upon a branch, he tumbled down from the tree and was killed. Bacchus bore the dead youth to the stars."[56]

Ampelos became the constellation *Vindemitor*, or the 'grape-gatherer.' In another version, Ampelos was killed while riding a bull maddened by the sting of a gadfly sent by Atë, the goddess of folly – the beast threw the boy and gored him to death. The Fates then granted Ampelos a second life as a vine, from the grapes of which Dionysos squeezed the first wine; Ampelos as a name literally means grape-vine. In a third version of the pair's

55 Pater, *Greek Studies*, 40.
56 Ovid, *Fasti*, iii, 407.

story, found in Nonnus' *Dionysiaca*, Ampelos was killed by Selene because he had challenged her.

A second male lover is recorded. According to several writers, Dionysos was guided during his journey to the underworld to rescue his mother Semele by a man called (variously) Hyplipnus, Prosymnus or Polymnus, who shamelessly requested, as his reward, to be Dionysos' lover. According to the version of the story told by the Christian writer Clement of Alexandria, Prosymnus died before Dionysos could honour his pledge, so to satisfy Prosymnus' spirit, Dionysos fashioned a phallus from a fig branch and sat on it at Prosymnus' tomb. This story survives in full only in a Christian source, the aim of which was very evidently to denigrate the pagan gods, but it appears to explain the origin of certain 'secret objects' that were used during the Dionysian mysteries.[57] Some scholars have suggested that the tale of the relationship with Prosymnus was invented to clarify why the rites involved a fig-wood phallus – rather than its presence being because of him. Whatever the reason, the fact remains that Dionysos was understood to have engaged in same-sex relations and this was not regarded as undesirable or ungodly – in fact, it was actively celebrated.

Over and above these two affairs, there is plenty of evidence in ancient texts that Dionysos was seen as effeminate or, perhaps, gender-fluid. In Euripides' *Bacchae* Pentheus describes the god as "this effeminate stranger" with fragrant golden curls. He continues: "Your body is not ill-formed, stranger, for women's purposes... For your hair is long, not through wrestling, scattered over your cheeks, full of desire; and you have a white skin from careful preparation, hunting after Aphrodite by your beauty not exposed to strokes of the sun, but beneath the shade."[58] The Athenian poet Callistratus described a statute of the young god by Praxiteles as having "the bloom of youth; it was full of daintiness,

57 Clement of Alexandria, *Exhortation to the Greeks* 2, 30.

58 Euripides, *Bacchae*, 235, 350 & 455.

it melted with desire..." Ovid called Dionysos "as pretty as a girl." Perhaps it is in this context that we are to understand a line in Roman poet Catullus' poem *Of Berecynthia and Attis* in which he asks "I, to be maenad: a part of myself: a sterile man?"[59]

Diodorus Siculus has similar things to say about the god:

> "Dionysus... was a man who was effeminate in body and altogether delicate; in beauty, however, he far excelled all other men and was addicted to indulgence in the delights of love...
>
> ... at festive gatherings in time of peace he wore garments which were bright-coloured and luxurious in their effeminacy.
>
> He was thought to have two forms, men say, because there were two Dionysoi, the ancient one having a long beard, because all men in early times wore long beards, the younger one being youthful and effeminate and young, as we have mentioned before."[60]

What's more, sex role reversal performed in honour of the deity may well have been part of the Dionysian rites. In Euripides' *Bacchae,* certainly, three men dress up as women in order to participate in a festival, putting on dresses because these are 'appropriate' to the event. Whether this is disguise or is expected is not entirely clear, but at least one of the men seems to derive considerable pleasure from appearing in drag.[61]

Part of the explanation of all of this may be that, according to the Greek writer now called Pseudo-Apollodorus "Hermes took him [the new-born Dionysos] to Ino and Athamas, and persuaded them to bring him up as a girl." The result of this childhood was, according to Roman playwright Seneca, that the boy looked like "a pretended maiden with golden ringlets, with saffron girdle

59 Callistratus, *Descriptions*, 8; Ovid, *Metamorphoses*, 3, 664.
60 Diodorus, *Historia Biblioteca*, 4.4.2, 4.4.4 & 4.5.2.
61 Euripides, *Bacchae*, 925-45.

binding thy garments. So thereafter this soft vesture has pleased thee, folds loose hanging and the long-trailing mantle." Nonnus added that "he moulded his lips to speak in a girlish voice, tied a scented veil on his hair. He put on all a woman's many coloured garments: fastened a maiden's vest about his chest and the firm circle of his bosom, and fitted a purple girdle over his hips like a band of maidenhood." Hence, apparently uniting two of the god's attributes, Philostratus the Elder, wrote: "if you look at the vine-sprays woven together and at the clusters hanging from them and how the grapes stand out one by one, you will certainly hymn Dionysos and speak of the vine as 'queenly giver of grapes.'"[62]

So it was that, as an adult, "dainty Bacchus does not blush to sprinkle with perfume his flowing locks, nor in his soft hand to brandish the slender thyrsos, when with mincing gait he trails his robe gay with barbaric gold." For some, as a consequence, it inevitably followed that the god's sexuality was affected: in Aristophanes' play, *The Frogs*, Herakles asks Dionysos "Were you loved [physically] by a man?" something to which he responds in the affirmative. Amongst other myths linking Dionysos to gay sexuality are an episode in the *Fables of Aesop* during which Dionysos gets Prometheus drunk, and then creates homosexuals while moulding mankind from clay.[63]

Straight Dionysos

Dionysos had a large number of heterosexual partners as well as the two male lovers. One of the complaints made against the god in the *Bacchae* is that "He is with the young girls day and night, alluring them with joyful mysteries."[64]

Most famously, when, after defeating the Minotaur, Theseus abandoned Cretan princess Ariadne asleep on Naxos, Dionysos

62 Pseudo-Apollodorus, *Bibliotheca* 3.28; Seneca, *Oedipus*, 418; Nonnus, *Dionysiaca*, 14.143; Philostratus, *Imagines*, 1.31.

63 Seneca, *Hercules Furens*, 472; Aristophanes, *Frogs*, 57.

64 Euripides, *Bacchae*, 235.

found and married her. Another account claims that Dionysos ordered Theseus to abandon Ariadne on the island, for he had glimpsed her whilst Theseus carried her onto the ship and had decided to marry her. The couple had as many as five children together. All the accounts end with Ariadne's tragic early death, but the relationship was a happy one – as Robert Graves depicted: his Ariadne "calls a blessing down… Playing the queen to nobler company" [than the faithless Theseus].[65]

The children born of the relationship with Ariadne are just a few of the offspring that have been allotted to the young god-although accounts vary widely on the number and the identities of the mothers. Some of his children were divine, arising from affairs with various goddesses. These the titan-huntress Aura was mother of twins with Dionysos; Telete, goddess of initiation into the Dionysian mysteries, was daughter of a nymph, Nikaia, who was made drunk and then raped in her sleep by the god. The oceanid nymph Periboea was similarly ravished by Dionysos whilst she slept. The three Graces, Methe, the nymph of drunkenness, Thysa, nymph of the frenzy of the orgy and Pasithea, who became wife of Hypnos, god of sleep, are all said to be descended from Dionysos.

One of these divine relationships was an especially significant one. Aphrodite's cult had links with those of Dionysos-Bacchus and the goddess was said to have been his lover, appropriate given that each of them was a deity of fertility. Together they are said to have been the parents of Hymenaeus, the god of weddings and of Iacchus, god of the Eleusinian Mysteries. Priapus was reputed to be another of their sons, although this was a symbolic as much as literal descent, in that "people filled with wine are naturally excited to amorous pleasures."[66]

As for mortal children, a number of kings, princesses, lords and other distinguished figures were said to have been sired by

65 Robert Graves, *Theseus & Ariadne*.
66 Eusebius, *The Preparation of the Gospels*, 2.2.5.

Dionysos with noble women. One such was Physkoa, from Orthia in Elis, who is remembered as one of the founders of his cult in that city. Their son was Narcaeus, who became the first priest of Dionysos in Elis.

There were also briefer couplings which did not lead to children. For example, it's recorded that Dionysos seduced a young woman at Artemis' sanctuary at Karai. He was also involved with Pallene, princess of Sithonia in Thrace, and with several nymphs, amongst them Kronois. Equally, the handsome youth could attract women even if he wasn't interested in them: Psalacantha, a nymph, failed to win the love of Dionysos in preference to Ariadne, and ended up being changed into a plant. Equally, Dionysos fell for the nymph Beroe, from Beirut in Phoenicia; struck by arrows fired by Eros, he "scanned the tender body of the longhaired maiden, full of admiration," but ultimately was disappointed, as she married Poseidon.[67]

One story of the origin of the vine concerns one of Dionysos' heterosexual relationships. It's said that he visited a man called Oeneus and fell for his wife, Althaea. When Oeneus realised this had happened, he left their home on the pretext of performing sacred rites, allowing the couple to be together. In recognition of Oeneus' noble generosity, Dionysos gave him the vine and showed him how to cultivate it, declaring that its fruit should be called 'oinos' from the name of his host.[68]

Stories such as those of the passion for Beroe and the disreputable rape of Nikaia indicate that Dionysos was certainly not indifferent to women. Perhaps the best summary is to say that the Greeks were perfectly at ease with the idea of a bisexual god, one who simply followed his inclinations and attractions as the opportunity arose, and thought no more of it than that.

---

67 Nonnus, *Dionysiaca* 42.

68 Pseudo-Hyginus, *Fabulae* 274.

DRAMA & POETRY

Performance art and drama were central to the god's worship and several of his festivals involved dramatic performances and poetry competitions. These events were the initial driving force behind the development of theatre.[69]

As we saw at the start, one of Dionysos' by-names was *Melpomenos*, taken from the muse of drama. As well as his constant links with Pan and his satyrs, then, the god was associated with the Muses, symbolic of his roles as the patron god and inspirer of the drama arts and as the protector of theatres.

Two forms of verse are particularly associated with the Dionysian cult; these are the *dithyrambos* and *phallophoreion* hymn types. The former is especially renowned. The meaning of the name is lost but from the earliest times it was connected to the choral worship of Dionysos. Verses were probably improvised by priests during the frenzy of the god's ceremonies, as a result of which there was no fixed metre or structure; instead, it was irregular, wild poetry – albeit occasionally accompanied by music.

In time, the dithyramb evolved into a recognised form of lyric, a style distinguished by being impetuous and passionate. An example is Leigh Hunt's 1825 translation of Francesco Redi's *Baccho in Toscana* (*Bacchus in Tuscany – a Dithyrambic Poem*), a hymn to wine that concludes in terms that will, by now, be familiar:

> "At these glad sounds,
> The Nymphs, in giddy rounds,
> Shaking their ivy diadems and grapes,
> Echoed the triumph in a thousand shapes.
> The Satyrs would have joined them; but alas!
> They couldn't; for they lay about the grass,
> As drunk as apes."

---

69 X. Riu, *Dionysism & Comedy*, 1999, 104–106.

IDENTIFICATION WITH OTHER GODS

Dionysos' origins and parentage are complex and his nature can seem like a confusing combination of traits and connections. This is only compounded by the overlap that exists between him and other, ostensibly separate, gods.

Iakkhos & Zagreus

In the Eleusinian Mysteries Dionysos was identified with Iacchus, who was reputed to be the son or, alternatively, the husband of Demeter (who, it may be recalled, was also known as Dionysos' first mother). Iacchus appears to have been a native Greek god who shared some characteristics with Dionysos and whose worship was subsumed within the cult of the Thracian newcomer.

As early as the fifth century BCE, the two gods became combined. Certainly, they shared several common traits- for example, they both claimed to have been brought up on Mount Nysa, they both had bull's horns and Iacchus too had "attendant thyiads" who danced in "night-long frenzy."[70]

As a result, in Euripides' *Bacchae* (of around 405 BCE), the bacchantes are described as beginning to "wave the thyrsos ... calling on Iacchus, the son of Zeus, Bromius, with united voice." Iacchus was sometimes known as the 'third' Dionysos, the incarnation that followed the first Dionysos Zagreus, son of Persephone, and the second, the son of Semele.[71]

Later, the geographer Strabo recorded that the Greeks gave "the name Iacchus not only to Dionysos but also to the leader-in-chief of the mysteries," that is, to the priest who led the rites in the guise of the god. In addition, Iacchus was identified with the Dionysos of the Orphic mysteries.[72]

70 Sophocles, *Antigone*, 1115–1125 & 1146–1154; fragment 959.
71 *Bacchae*, 725; Nonnus, *Dionysiaca*, 48.962–968.
72 Strabo, 10.3.10.

To add to this confusion, the story is told about an individual named Zagreus who was also said to be son of Zeus and Persephone (like the 'first' Dionysos). It is again uncertain whether Zagreus was just another name for Dionysos or whether he was a separate individual; for example, Aeschylus identified him as really being Hades/Pluto, in which case he might effectively be Dionysos' step-father (see below, too). For Walter Pater, it was partly the figure of Zagreus that introduced a note of sadness into Dionysos' cult.[73]

Osiris

According to the Greek understanding of the Egyptian pantheon, Dionysos was regularly equated with Osiris. There were several grounds for this. Osiris was the offspring of the union of sky and earth; he was a personification of the corn, dying and being reborn from year to year; he also was the first to teach men to cultivate corn – just as Dionysos did with the vine. Osiris was – in some versions – a tree spirit and, most notably, like Dionysos he went through a process of dismemberment by antagonists, pieces of his body being scattered far and wide. This is thought to symbolise the scattering of seed or the winnowing of harvested grain (just as Dionysos was symbolised by a winnowing fan). The mangling of Osiris' body was then followed by its re-assembly and resurrection. The Apis bull was seen as an intermediary between humans and Osiris; in later times the sacred bull combined with Osiris to create Serapis, who was regarded as an incarnation of the deity himself. In this form, he was the major deity worshipped by the Greek Ptolemies; Dionysos' links to bulls have already been described.

According to Diodorus Siculus, as early as the fifth century BCE, the two gods had been syncretised into a single deity who was known as Dionysos-Osiris. Dionysos-Osiris was particularly

73 Pater, *Greek Studies*, 43.

popular in Ptolemaic Egypt, because the Ptolemies simultaneously claimed descent from Dionysos whilst as pharaohs they came of the lineage of Osiris. These associations were most visible during a deification ceremony in which Roman general Mark Antony became Dionysos-Osiris and his partner Cleopatra became the living embodiment of Isis-Aphrodite.

Hades

The Greek philosopher Heraclitus, unifying opposites, declared that Hades, the lord of the underworld, and Dionysos, the very essence of indestructible life, are in fact one and the same god. The reason for this proposal seems to be that, at the festival of the Phallophoria, phalli were paraded about in honour of the Hades and songs were addressed to him. Given the fact that the phallus is an obvious symbol of vitality, Heraclitus concluded that Hades was none other than "the same as Dionysos, for whom they rave and act like bacchantes."

Hades may in fact have functioned as a pseudonym for the underworld Dionysos. It has been further suggested that this dual identity may have been one of the secrets revealed to those who were inducted into the Dionysian Mysteries. As we saw earlier, one of the epithets of Dionysos was 'Chthonios,' meaning 'the subterranean;' another was 'the gaping one,' comparing him to death that ultimately swallows up all mortal beings.

The possible links between the two gods seem to be confirmed by the facts that there was considerable death symbolism in Dionysian worship and that some statues of Dionysos closely resemble those of Hades. Both gods were, in turn, associated with a divine tripartite form of Zeus and he, like his son Dionysos, was occasionally believed to have an underworld form, closely identified with Hades, to the point that they were occasionally thought of as being identical. This web of connections all ties in with the idea of Persephone as Dionysos' mother, with whom he is sometimes shown taking the place of Hades/Pluto.

Christianity

Numerous scholars have compared narratives surrounding the Christian figure of Jesus with those associated with Dionysos. Both experienced death and resurrection; both endured a trial (Dionysos before King Pentheus on charges of claiming divinity, an episode that is directly comparable to the story of Jesus before Pontius Pilate).

The Dionysian cult had developed into a strict monotheism by the fourth century CE. Together with Mithraism and other sects, the cult formed an instance of pagan monotheism that stood in direct competition with Early Christianity during Late Antiquity. It seems highly probable that the Dionysian cult and its history, with its ideas of suffering, purification and rebirth, influenced early Christianity, especially the way in which Christians conceived of themselves as a 'new' or 'foreign' religion centred around a saviour deity.

As we shall see in Part Two, the parallels between Dionysos and Jesus still have resonance in modern times, with Aleister Crowley emphasising how each were manifestations of a very deep religious and psychological concept of spiritual and physical rebirth.

Cult & Worship

> "We must not be surprised if in honour of Dionysus fire is crowned by earth, for the earth will take part with fire in the Bacchic revel and will make it possible for the revellers to take wine from springs and to draw milk from clods of earth or from a rock as from living breasts. Listen to Pan, how he seems to be hymning Dionysus... as he dances an Evian fling."[74]

Critic Walter Pater summarised the Dionysian cult wonderfully. He understood how the god "recalled to the Greek mind, under a single imaginable form, an outward body of flesh presented to the senses, and comprehending, as its animating soul, a whole world of thoughts, surmises, greater and less experiences." In short, "the religion of Dionysus was, for those who lived in it, a complete religion, a complete sacred representation and interpretation of the whole of life."[75]

The worship of Dionysos was a celebration by the entire earth-not just men and women, but all the elements of the natural world and the lesser divinities too. It represented a universal rite. Its purpose was both dramatic and magical: it aimed to bring about the regeneration of plants and the reproduction of animals through the symbolic re-enactment of the god's sufferings, death and rebirth. He was a god who had miraculously overcome death and had been resurrected.

Wine already played an important role in Greek culture, but the cult of Dionysos became the principal religious focus involving and explaining its consumption. As we've already explored, wine, as well as the vines and grapes that produce it, were seen as not

---

74 Philostratus, *Imagines*, 1.14.1.
75 Pater, *Greek Studies*, 10 & 18.

only a gift from the god, but as a symbolic incarnation of him on earth.

The Dionysian cult gave structure and meaning to wine drinking, so that, rather than being a god of drunkenness (as he was often stereotyped in the post-Classical era), the religion of Dionysos centred on the correct consumption of wine, possibly mixed with other psychoactive ingredients such as poppy. The aim of this was easing suffering, bringing joy and, for initiates, inspiring a divine madness as distinct from a helpless drunkenness. Inebriation, along with wild dancing, facilitated celebrants' sensation that they were being possessed by or assimilated with their god- the ecstasy or enthusiasm mentioned at the start of the book.

The cult was also a cult of souls: the maenads nourished the dead with milk, wine, honey, water and offerings of blood, and the god himself facilitated communication back and forth between the living and the dead. Hence, he is sometimes categorised as a dying-and-rising god.[76]

Last, but definitely not least, Dionysos is an agriculture and vegetation deity. His connections to wine, grape-harvest, orchards and vegetation all demonstrate his primary or original role as a nature god.

THYRSOS

Essential to all celebrations of Dionysos was his thyrsos or wand. Anyone who participated in a Dionysian rite might be termed a 'thyrsos-bearer' although this was consciously contrasted with the status of initiates to the god's mysteries, the *bakkhoi*.

The thyrsos (or thyrsus) was a stout fennel staff, tipped with a pine-cone and decorated with ribbons and ivy; sometimes, it was dipped in honey. It was (and still is) carried by bacchantes

76 X. Riu, *Dionysism & Comedy*, 1999, 104–106.

and maenads at the head of their rapturous processions whilst they sing hymns, shout for joy and dance in the god's honour. According to Euripides, there was a distinctive dance step that was performed with the wand: "you must hold it in your right hand and raise your right foot in unison with it." The thyrsos as staff, or sceptre, was struck on the ground to summon followers and, perhaps, to beat time: "as when Dionysus strikes his thyrsos his followers rush riotous to the dance… keeping time to the call of the rhythm." "Haste, haste hither with nimble-footed pace, let us sing Sparta, the city that delights in choruses divinely sweet and graceful dances, when our maidens bound lightly by the river side, like frolicsome fillies, beating the ground with rapid steps and shaking their long locks in the wind, as bacchantes wave their wands in the wild revels of the wine-god."[77]

It appears that the thyrsos could also be used as a goad to drive the bacchantes along. Philostratus said as much: "Dionysus himself stands where he can watch them, puffing out his cheeks with passion and applying the Bacchic goad to the women."[78]

Furthermore, the god's staff or wand had miraculous powers-it operated as a conduit for the god's own magic: "one took her thyrsos and struck it into a rock, and forth there gushed a limpid spring; and another plunged her wand into the lap of earth and there the god sent up a fount of wine; and all who wished for draughts of milk had but to scratch the soil with their finger-tips and there they had it in abundance…" According to a second account, "Another struck the thirsty soil with the point of a thyrsos; the top of the hill split at once, and the hard rock poured out purple wine of itself, or with a tap on the rock fountains of milk ran out of themselves in white streams." This might go to explain why the staff might in turn be offered to Dionysos: "A triple gift did Biton dedicate under the greenwood tree, to Pan a

77 Euripides, *Bacchae*, 944; Julian the Emperor, *Letters*, 74; Aristophanes, *Lysistrata*, 1247.
78 Philostratus, *Imagines*, 1.18.2.

goat, roses to the nymphs, and a thyrsos to Bacchus. Receive with joy his gifts, you gods, and increase, Pan, his flock, you nymphs his fountain, and Bacchus his cellar."[79]

The creation of fountains of milk and wine is not just a matter of magic and feasting, though. Firstly, it is symbolic of the fecundity and generosity associated with the god, hence one Greek writer's lush evocation of "choruses of bacchantes, and rocks flowing with wine, and nectar dripping from clusters of grapes, and the earth enriching the broken soil with milk."[80]

Secondly, it was the realm of the dead that was traditionally furnished with such bounty, so that in making such wonders appear on the earth surface, Dionysos was creating a literal heaven on earth, symbolically repeating his journey to the underworld to rescue his mother Semele and bring her back to life. This is part of the reason for the disordered and ecstatic nature of his rites – they are breaking down the barriers between dimensions. This is precisely why the author Philodamus of Scarphea praised the god – not only can he inaugurate a "blessed era of prosperity" but, "for mortals from their pains, you have opened a haven without toils."[81]

So sacred and revered was the staff that oaths would be made upon it. Nonnus recorded one such solemn vow: "I swear it by Dionysos, who has touched my board, I swear it by your thyrsos, and by Aphrodite of the sea."[82]

As a symbol of the god, the waving and whirling of the thyrsos was directly responsible (in part at least) for the ecstatic state that descended upon celebrants – making them "thyrsos-wild." The women would become crazed and would howl, "hair flowing, like a maenad roused by the thyrsos" for, "when my mind's inspired, stirred by the leafy thyrsos, the spirit is lifted

79 Euripides, *Bacchae*, 704; Nonnus, *Dionysiaca*, 45.289; *Greek Anthology* Book 6, Sabinus Grammaticus, 6.158.
80 Philostratus, *Imagines*, 1.18.1.
81 Philodamus, *Paean to Dionysus*.
82 Nonnus, *Dionysiaca*, 33.365.

above mortal suffering." Seemingly, merely seeing the staff had an effect comparable to ingesting drugs: "The thyrsos fails to aid you, chewing laurels for me..." Even the rod's owner was not immune to its powers – Dionysos was said to have "mingled thyrsos-mad with the Bacchant women upon the hills."[83]

In addition to be being a symbol of peace and prosperity, the thyrsos was often used like a weapon. Although we saw earlier that the fennel stem was chosen by Dionysos as a way of minimising the harm that blows from a thyrsos could cause, the staff could still be termed "man-breaking," "ship-destroying," "skin-piercing," "war-like" or "avenging." It may have been a 'woman's implement,' merely a stick wound with foliage, but it was pointed and sharp too – hence: "the Bacchant yelled in triumph, the Bassarid cast her vine-wreathed point, the heads of many men in that black-skin crowd were brought down by the womanish thyrsos." In consequence, the rods of the Bassarids are called "their bastard spears" and "leafy weapons of war."[84]

Pretty blatantly, though, the thyrsos is a phallic symbol, appropriate to the god's function as a bringer of fertility. The pine cone tip is modelled the glans of the penis, although at Corinth two entire statues to the god were carved from pine wood at the behest of the Delphic oracle. Dionysos is even called the "the thyrsos-lover" in one text, a phrase which surely must allude to his gay sexuality.[85] Perhaps, too, there is a sexual connotation in the thyrsos dripping with honey. Hence, Philostratus has "serpents stand erect, and thyrsos trees are dripping, *I think*, with honey" and Euripides described how "from every ivy-wreathed staff sweet rills of honey trickled."[86]

83 Ovid, *Tristia (Letters from Exile)*, 4.1.1; Ovid, *Art of Love*, 3.710; Ovid, *Letters from Pontus*, 2.5.41; Nonnus, *Dionysiaca*, 25.380 & 45.197.

84 Nonnus, *Dionysiaca*, 14.386, 20.197 & 29.201; Euripides, *Bacchae*, 748.

85 *Greek Anthology*, 3.1.

86 Philostratus, *Imagines*, 1.18.1; Euripides, *Bacchae*, 704.

WORSHIPPERS & RETINUE

The classical texts reveal that the god had two separate sets of followers. There was a host of minor divinities, who were associated with the god Pan, and there were mortal, female devotees. Strabo enumerated the young god's mixed entourage more fully, recording that, at festivals, "the sileni and satyri and sacchae, and also the lenae [a name related to Dionysos' epithet as treader of grapes] and thyiae and mimallones and naiades and nymphae and the beings called tityri, [were the ministers] of Dionysus." Mortals and immortals might all be jumbled together in Bacchus' raving rout.[87]

Satyrs & Nymphs

Eusebius recorded that Dionysos "leads about Satyrs with him, who afford him pleasure and delight in their dances and their goat-songs."[88] Originally, it appears that Dionysos was *only* accompanied by minor divinities. Usually, the sole females in the procession were nymphs of various descriptions (most especially dryads and hamadryads), although sometimes his mortal spouse Ariadne would appear alongside the god or the three graces might be present. The males were typically satyrs, the flute playing satyrs called *tityri* and the slightly older ones 'sileni.' These beings all tended to be marked by their exaggerated erections.

Silenus was said to be the son of Hermes (or Pan) and of a nymph. He became the companion and substitute father of Dionysus and he was often imagined as a fat, jolly man drinking wine in the company of satyrs. Whilst often intoxicated (or, perhaps, because of this) Silenus was also said to be able to see into the future.

---

87 Strabo, *Geography*, 10.3.10.

88 Eusebius, *The Preparation of the Gospels*, 2.2.4.

What's very noticeable is the fact that the pans, satyrs and sileni were all divine beings in part-goat form. This seems to underline not just Dionysos' own personal links with goats but his wild and woodland character. He was a god of trees as well as of crops – although, in fact, ancient myth didn't always hold these different plants strictly apart. Fauns were also felt to be responsible for crop growth, so that a key concept of the early cult emerges as being the promotion of fertility in vegetation of all descriptions. Dionysos' bull form merely seems to be another expression of his power over, concern and responsibility for, all forms of plant life and crops.[89]

Wild Women

> "your wanton initiates lead the mystic revels. Along with you a troop of bassarids in Edonian dance beat the ground… now amidst Cadmean dames has come a maenad, the impious comrade of Ogygian Bacchus, with sacred fawn-skins girt about her loins, her hand a light thyrsos brandishing. Their hearts maddened by you, the matrons have set their hair a-flowing…"[90]

As time passed, mortal women began to predominate as the celebrants in the god's rites. Despite this devotion, their reputation was often poor. In the *Bacchae,* King Pentheus complains that female adherents of the god "creep off different ways into secrecy to serve the beds of men, on the pretext that they are maenads worshipping – but they consider Aphrodite before Bacchus."[91] This general attitude to Dionysos' female followers was made manifest when a later writer pictured a man who was "followed by his ladyloves, like a cock by barnyard hens,

89 Pater, *Greek Studies*, 11–12 & 14

90 Seneca, *Oedipus*, 401. Edonis is a region in Thrace; Cadmos was king of Thebes; the Ogygian Bacchus was specially honoured in the same city.

91 Euripides, *Bacchae*, 224–225.

or a he-goat leading the she-goats of the herd, or like Semele's son Dionysos escorting the thyades, sobades, maenads, and bacchantes; only he did not put on a fawn skin and wear the saffron-coloured robe." 'Sobades' is Greek word that denotes an aggressive or overbearing woman, a female with loose morals or – at worst – a prostitute who openly pursued clients.[92]

Another illustration of the sometimes-low opinion of maenads is the story of Agave, who was the queen of Thebes and sister of Semele, the mother of Dionysos. She spitefully alleged that Zeus wasn't actually the boy's father, implying that her sister was not only a liar but had lax morals. Naturally, Dionysos wasn't happy to hear his mother's honour impugned, so he punished Agave by making her into a maenad so crazed that she dismembered her own son, Pentheus. It may seem contradictory to us that the deity's manner of punishment is to render his victim like his own followers but there's a cruel poetic justice to it as well.

The central feature of Dionysus' ceremonies, the 'bacchanals,' was that they were attended by delirious female participants. These women were called, variously, *maenads, bassarids, bacchae, bacchantes, thyiades, lenae, clodones* and *mimallones*. All the names denote the women's frantic state as they succumbed to the "god-possessed frenzy –" they would dance wildly, dressed in the skins of foxes and fawns, and would engage in ecstatic orgies.[93]

According to Athenaeus, the "Macedonian bacchants, the so-called 'mimallones,' 'bassarae' and 'Lydian women', [appeared] with hair streaming down and crowned with wreaths, some made of snakes, others of smilax [bindweed], vine-leaves and ivy; in their hands some held daggers, others snakes." The decorated hair seems to have typified them: "She plaited into her flower-decked hair the natural tendrils of the maddening ivy like a prophetess of the bassarids..." In their wild or raving state, it

92 Niketas Choniates, *Annals*, 321; S.D. Olson, *Fragmenta Comica-Eupolis, Fragmenta incertarum fabularum*, 2014, 102.

93 Philodamus, *Paean to Dionysus*.

was even possible that "thyrsos-bearing maenads [would] hunt the snake to twine about their hair." Serpents might also be used as girdles or belts, allegedly.[94]

The term 'maenad' was applied because the women would become mad or manic during the rites of the cult. Dionysos himself was sometimes referred to as *manikos,* the mad one, to underline the significance of altered states of consciousness in his worship. Later sources might still refer to these women as 'nymphs' but, by the time of Alexander the Great and his successors, this word had lost its sense of divinity and meant simply an ideal female of the Dionysian outdoors, a non-wild bacchante.

The name *thyiades* was used for the women because their madness was the result of being caught up with the spirit of the god – the term shares the same root as our present word 'enthused.' Music and dance helped get them worked up into the "mind-robbing throes of madness," as many writers tried to convey. "The battalions of bassarids also moved like a flood. As they gathered, one twined a rope of snakes about her head, one knotted her hair with scented ivy; another madly caught up her bronze-headed thyrsos, another let down loose tresses of long hair over her neck, a maenad unveiled, while the wind blew the unbound locks over her shoulders; another clapped the pair of brazen cymbals, and shook the ringlets upon her head; another, driven by the impulse of madness, beat the heavy booming drumskin with her hands, and sounded a loud echo of the battle-din." The women would howl, and foam at the mouth; they were mad eyed and would dance wildly: "Amid the roaring tumult, the bassarid in her rich garb shook the cymbals out of her hands, swung her feet round, shook off the yellow trusses of the stitched shoes from her paddling feet, while the windswept waves rose to the head of the swimming bacchant and drenched her curling hair." They wove their dances to the tones of pipes and horns

94 Athenaeus, *Deipnosophists*, 5.198; Nonnus, *Dionysiaca*, 8.6; Euripides, *Bacchae*, 99; Philostratus, *Imagines*, 2.17.7.

and the beat of rattles, tambourines (*tympana*), drums and feet: "Many a bassarid skipped about, tapping the floor with wild slipper; many a satyr stormed the resounding ground with heavy foot, and revelled with side-trippings of his tumbling feet as he rested an arm on the neck of some maddened bacchant." All these images, especially the loosing of hair and the casting off of shoes, indicate the women's escape from conventional behaviour.[95]

This dancing may often be referred to as 'raving,' but we should not lose sight of the fact that it was also exuberant, joyful and youthfully energetic. Euripides compared a dancer to "a fawn sporting in the green pleasures of the meadow," and described how "the Bacchante, rejoicing like a foal with its grazing mother, rouses her swift foot in a gambolling dance." The celebrations made older worshippers feel re-invigorated – a joy in itself.[96]

A key means of inducing the physical state of dislocation or elation was through movement. The maenads would whirl and shake their heads as they danced. The effect this produced was understood to be not a human but a divine madness – Dionysos was the raging god and the raving maenads partook of his condition. Additionally, a number of Dionysian festivals occurred in winter, and it has been suggested that the maenads resorted to high places in a cold season because the low temperatures further aided their ecstasies.[97]

Caught up in the frenzy, raw flesh was consumed, according to the poet Catullus: "In rapture his bacchantes raved madly, crazed in mind, with cries of 'euhoe' and tossing of heads; some brandished the thyrsos with hidden tip, some flourished the torn limbs of bullocks..." For the women to be persuaded to consume uncooked meat, it will be plain that through the rites they shared an overwhelming sensory experience. Catullus continued –

95 Nonnus, *Dionysiaca*, 43.331, 14.338, 15.146, 23.190, 40.225 & 47.273; Euripides, *Bacchae*, 735–770.

96 Euripides, *Bacchae*, 865, 165 & 189–190.

97 J. Bremmer, 'Otto's Dionysus (1933),' in Bernabe, *Redefining Dionysos*, 2013, 15; also 171 & 181; Plutarch, *De primo frigido*, c.18, 953 D.

"some wreathed themselves with twining snakes, some celebrated the secret rites of the hollow box, rights they wished the profane to hear in vain: others beat the drums with the flat of their hands, or raised a clear ringing from rounded cymbals: they blew endless strident calls on the horns and the barbarous flute shrilled with fearful tunes." In another account, we are told how a young participant called Evanthe "transferred her hand from the unsteady service of the thyrsos to the steady service of the wine-cup, dedicated to Bacchus her whirling tambourine that stirred the rout of the bacchants to fury, this dappled spoil of a flayed fawn, her clashing brass corybantic cymbals, her green thyrsos surmounted by a pine-cone, her light, but deeply-booming drum, and the winnowing-basket she often carried raised above her snooded hair."[98]

There is, in the various records and descriptions, some indication that the female celebrants had sex with each other as part of their ceremonies. The rites seem to have been (intentionally) highly arousing, so this would hardly be surprising. As well as needing relief from the tensions brought about by the celebrations, it might be thought only apt to pay respect to the gay god in this way. In the *Bacchae,* Euripides has King Pentheus plan to spy on the women "in the grips of love" together in the bushes. Even if this interpretation is mistaken, the women might have been going off to masturbate alone, thereby underlining the fundamental sexual element of the rites.[99]

Any sexual elements notwithstanding, the primary emotions stirred by the ceremonies were invocation of and devotion to the god. One author wrote how each celebrant "loves Dionysos [and] fashions his image in her mind and pictures him and sees him, absent though he is; for though the look of the bacchante's eyes is wavering, yet assuredly it is not free from dreams of love."[100]

---

98 Catullus, *Poems*, 64.250; *Greek Anthology* Book 6, Phalaecus, 6.165.
99 Euripides, *Bacchae*, 957.
100 Philostratus, *Imagines*, 2.17.7.

The Dionysian rites deliberately involved intense physical and mental exertion coupled with sleep deprivation: these were designed in combination to generate the necessary physical and mental exhaustion that could precipitate a trance-like state. The dancing was furious and the women would "tread where garlands sway from many an unguent-vase; in mazy rounds our languid limbs shall know disport; by step, by garb, by voice, each shall play the quivering maenad." Certainly, by the climax of their ceremonies, the women would have ended up exhausted and somewhat distraught, "Your trembling limbs prostrate, you maenads, low upon the ground."[101] Even so, not all may have derived deep religious experience from the ceremonies. As Plato said, "the thyrsos-bearers are many, but the mystics few." Nevertheless, perhaps the excitement, exertion and sex were enough of a shared religious experience for most.[102]

Once enthused, these raging women could be driven to almost superhuman feats. Addressing Bacchus, Horace called him "master of naiads, of bacchae owning the power to uproot the tallest ash-trees with their bare hands." Far worse than this might happen though: the women had a reputation for accosting and assaulting anyone or anything unlucky enough to stray into their path. "Thereat we fled, to escape being torn into pieces by the bacchantes; but they, with hands that bore no weapon of steel, attacked our cattle as they browsed." Any creature – livestock large or small and even human beings – that came across the raving women might be in mortal peril: "'Well then sister,' gentle Panthia replied 'why not grab him first and like bacchantes tear him limb from limb, or tie him up at least and cut his balls off?"[103]

101 *Greek Anthology*, Book 16, Planudean, 289; Sidonius Apollinaris, *Letters*, 9.13.5; Euripides, *Bacchae*, 578.

102 Plato, *Phaedo*, 69.

103 Horace, *Odes*, 3.25; Euripides, *Bacchae*, 720; Plautius, *Casina*, 5, 4; Palaephatus, *On Unbelievable Things*, 33; Apuleius, *Golden Ass (Metamorphoses)*, 1.13; also, Athenaeus, *Deipnosophists*, 12.40.

Although the holy ecstasy may have justified the dismemberment of livestock and the consumption of its raw flesh, it seems clear that the women occasionally indulged in less religiously motivated activities. They engaged in rushing, breakneck hunts with the god, they rampaged around districts looting or scaring inhabitants, or they became so frenzied and ravening that they would even get into fights without feeling fear – although it has been suggested that when this happened, the maenads were motivated more by blind fury than by valour. Pope Dionysius of Alexandria recorded that "There is a certain spectacular place beside the fair-flowing Ganges, a place which is revered and sacred, where Bacchus once walked in anger, when the delicate fawn-skins of the Lenae were turned into shields, and their thyrsoi were changed into iron, and their belts and the tendrils of the twisting vine into the coils of serpents, then when in their folly they slighted the festival of the god." Rather like berserkers, the frenzied women felt benumbed and invulnerable: "Nothing shakes the bassarids; strike them with axe or two-edged sword, they remain unwounded."[104]

The frenzy of the maenads has been described as a collective religious hysteria, a process that gave the participants unusual strength and aggression and which made them invulnerable to injury. The reports of the maenads' behaviour may be exaggerated but they do not appear to be fictional. A combination of excitement, intoxication, exertion and exhaustion do indeed seem to have produced a heightened mental state in which the women were temporarily rendered insensible to fear and pain-meaning, for example, that they could handle snakes, carry fire or run across rocky ground barefoot.[105]

In conclusion – although both sexes worshipped Dionysos and were initiated into his mysteries, it's clear that women had

104 Augustine, *City of God*, Book 18, 18.13; Nonnus, *Dionysiaca*, 39.80, 30.1 & 46.79; Dionysius of Alexandria, *Guide to the Inhabited World*, 1150.

105 J. Bremmer, 'Greek Maenadism Reconsidered' in *Zeitschrift für Papyrologie und Epigraphie* vol.55, 1984, 267–272; Nonnus, *Dionysiaca*, 14, 384.

a very special place in his cult. This status is underlined by the fact that in the city of Brysiai in Lacedaemon, there was a temple of Dionysos which contained an image that only women were permitted see and before which women by themselves performed secret sacrificial rites.[106]

THE RITES OF DIONYSOS

"Chaste and holy are the rites of Dionysus"[107]

In discussing the worship of Dionysos, it must be stressed at the outset that there was no formalised religion or 'order of service.' There was no holy book around which the cult focused and, as devotion to the god was spread across the whole of the ancient world, from the Middle East as far as Spain, there were no standardised or common practices.

Dionysos has been described as a gatekeeper or master of altered states of being. Through the intake of certain substances in a religious or ceremonial context, he was able to make his presence felt in the hearts of his devotees. The worshippers' souls temporarily merged with the divine and experienced the joys and terrors of that existence; they also merged with those of their fellow worshippers. The god's ecstasy was a mass phenomenon that was all about surrender to the him – abandoning your daily identity and becoming mad – albeit it in a divine, positive and wholesome manner. The use of masks in the god's rites symbolised this merger.[108]

The religion of Dionysos frequently incorporated rituals that required the wearing of wooden masks. Some sources show the god himself participating in the rituals in the form of a masked and clothed pillar, pole, or tree. It has been argued that this

106 Pausanias, *Description of Greece*, 3, 20, 3.
107 Ariadne in R C Trevelyan's *Bride of Dionysos*, 1912.
108 R. Taylor-Perry, *Dionysos – The God Who Comes*, 2003, 6.

presence of masks in the rites has a very deep significance. There is no unmasked Dionysos and so, by extension, we are all Dionysos wearing a mask. We are identical with him and, as such, our journey towards self-knowledge involves peeling away successive masks.[109]

The central role of ecstasy in the deity's cult is quite unique, "with the result that Dionysos almost acquires a monopoly over enthusiasm and ecstasy." This aspect of his worship is something which can be especially attractive to modern audiences, but it should be recalled that in classical times, it had a dual nature. Sometimes the religious frenzy led to tragedy, with individuals such as Orpheus and Pentheus being torn limb from limb by the crazed maenads. Nonetheless, it was, too, a divine experience of liberating and purifying fulfilment and bliss. Plato, in *Phaedrus,* called the madness a divine gift.[110]

Maenadism

The major festivals tended to follow an established pattern. They would begin with groups of women processing out of the town or city where they lived, an event often accompanied by sacrifices. The handling of raw meat that these involved signified that a period of disruption and inversion of customary norms was beginning and the women were about to become 'maenads' for a time. Led by a priestess, the women marched off to nearby mountains (a process called *oreibasia*), where they would put on fawn skins, loosen their hair, and remove their shoes in advance of the rites. A certain equality of appearance among the group was produced by this; distinctions of class were erased to some extent by the uniform ritual garment, a transformation which at the same time liberated them from some of the formalities of social convention.

109 Anderson, *Masks of Dionysos – A Commentary on Plato's Symposium*, 1993, 7.
110 Burkert, *Greek Religion*, 110; Santamaria, in *Redefining Dionysos*, 48; Plato, *Phaedrus*, 244a.

Initially, the participants would prepare calmly and joyfully, sitting around singing hymns as they constructed their wreaths and staffs. We have a few words from one of these hymns preserved for us: the celebrants "being covered with the skins of young hinds and waving their thyrsi in their hands, sing a hymn, of which these are part of the words, 'When wisdom all in vain must be, then be not wise at all'."[111]

There would also be the sacrifice of specially made cakes. Then the main ceremony began, comprising music from drums and pipes, torch-light and vigorous dancing that involved leaping, head-shaking and gyrations. All of this, as well as sleep deprivation, cold and hunger, helped to induce a trance-like state. In due course, the women would collapse one by one and, when they had recovered sufficiently, they were possessed by a sense of euphoria.

In fact, involvement in these bacchic rites tended to be restricted to certain groups and to certain periods of time (in winter, every other year). In Greece, the city states (and often the women's husbands) were involved in regulating the ceremonies. It should be noted that, for all its reputation as the birthplace of democracy, classical Greece was a male-dominated and repressive society in which women's rights were highly circumscribed. The Dionysian rites offered its female celebrants rare opportunities to go out and to mix alone, albeit temporarily. They therefore provided a unique forum for independence and self-expression. The maenads represented psychic and physical freedom- a different mode of living and feeling for women.

Working themselves up into a frenzy might seem an undignified way for high-ranking women to behave, but it was clearly something that was seen to have a social and spiritual function within communities. Cities sanctioned these actions and, more significantly, other women apparently approved and

111 Euripides, *Bacchae*, 1043; Pseudo-Plutarch, *Names of Rivers and Mountains*, 001.3

respected them. The story is told of events in 350BC when some maenads at Amphissa collapsed exhausted in the city streets after a Dionysian rite. There were soldiers present in the city who might have taken advantage and molested the sleepers, so other women of the city assembled to watch over the celebrants whilst they slept and then accompanied them safely to their homes.[112]

Drink & Drugs

As we well know, Bacchus/ Dionysos is primarily the god of the vine and it is unquestionable that drinking wine was a key part of his rites and a major contributor to the frenzy or elation that celebrants experienced. However, fermented grape juice alone may not have contributed to this. There are suggestions that opium or cannabis may have been mixed with the drink in some form.

British poet Robert Graves went even further in arguing for a psychotropic aspect to the ceremonies. In his 'historical grammar of poetic myth,' *The White Goddess* (1961), he proposed that there was a "secret Dionysiac mushroom cult." The god's companions, the centaurs, satyrs and maenads, all partook of the spotted toadstool, *Amanita muscaria*, which bestowed transcendental visions and "gave them enormous strength, erotic power, delirious visions and the gift of prophecy." It was this psycho-active fungus that was the true ambrosia consumed by the gods. Graves bolstered his argument by suggesting that those engaged in the Orphic and Eleusinian mysteries may have taken the small dung mushroom *panaeolus papilinionaceus,* which is similar in effect to mescalin (as Aleister Crowley may have understood – see later). It was the strength derived from mushroom intoxication that gave the maenads their ability to tear men and beasts limb from limb – not something they might have achieved drunk on wine alone. Graves also suggested that the

112 Plutarch, *De mulierum virtutibus*, c.13, 249E.

autumn Dionysiac festival of 'Mysterion' derived its name from the word *mykosterion* – the 'sprouting of toadstools.' He further suggested that wine gradually displaced mushrooms as the drug of choice at bacchanals.[113]

Sex

Although, as has been mentioned, the phallus was central to the cult and festivals of Dionysos, the god himself was never shown with an erection (although satyrs were). It is generally assumed – given our modern associations with the word orgy – that sex was absolutely central to Dionysian rites, but by and large this does not seem to have been the case. The delirium of the bacchae and maenads was not a sexual frenzy; eroticism was not a route to divine possession. The reason that Dionysos was manifested by and through the penis was instead to do with the fact that the phallus stood as a symbol of the god's omnipotence and vital force. It was a natural, rather than a pornographic, motif. In this connection it's worth adding that in the literature and imagery Dionysos' mortal retinue is comprised not of nubile young nymphs but of mature women; this in itself seems to make it clear that – symbolically as well as practically – the frenzy of the maenads is about something more than sex.[114]

This is not to say, all the same, that sex was absent from the cult. The divine Dionysos was a sexual being, for one thing, and, along with Eros, he was the "spirit of life and of life's ecstasy." The god's festivals originated in rural and agrarian feasts and their function in promoting fertility at the same time gave a licence for sexual expression. They were, too, events in which both sexes participated. In Euripides' play *The Bacchae*, King Pentheus complains to Dionysos that his nocturnal rites encourage immoral behaviour by women. Interestingly, the god replies to the effect

113 Graves, *The White Goddess*, 45, 99, 184 & 334.

114 Sissa & Detienne, *The Daily Life of the Greek Gods*, 2000, 231 & 236.

that identical things could happen in daylight too. In other words, he doesn't deny the accusation; he merely acknowledges that a certain amount of sexual freedom might well be enjoyed – but suggests that it was not essential to worship. To repeat, sex might well have followed the frenzies, in order to release accumulated tensions, but it was not necessarily seen as a vehicle or technique by which to contact the god.[115]

The evidence of pottery and sculpture shows that the god was patron of public displays of sexuality – couples might engage in intercourse in front of others, for example at *symposia* – drinking parties. It also appears that some initiations into the mysteries involved sexual intercourse, frequently between those already members of the cult with the newcomers (in other words, generally older with younger celebrants). The Dionysia festival celebrated every four years at Brauron, in Attica, involved drinking and the presence of many prostitutes for sex. Hence this line from Aristophanes – "what a fine, big four-year-festival arse she has." Other feasts for the god are known to have included scurrilous speeches and lascivious dances. For example, the first century CE prophet, Apollonius of Tyana, criticised the behaviour of Athenians during the Anthestria festival because he had seen men dancing in the guise of the *horai* (seasons), nymphs, or as bacchae, which he condemned as "soft [and] of effeminate tendency." We shall see other examples of sexual aspects to festivals shortly.[116]

Sacrifice

In Gaul the Samnites were reported by the geographer Strabo to worship a god whom he equated with Dionysos. He described how there was:

115 R. Kraemer, 'Ecstasy & Possession – the Attraction of Women to the Cult of Dionysus,' in *Harvard Theological Review*, vol.72, 1979, 60 & 68; Euripides, *Bacchae*, 314–318 & 485.

116 P. McGinty, *Interpretation & Dionysos*, 2013, 84; C. Isler-Kerenyi, *Dionysos in Archaic Greece*, 2007, 196; Burkert, *Greek Religion*, 109.

> "a small island, not very far out to sea, situated off the outlet of the River Leigeros; and the island is inhabited by the women of the Samnites, and they are possessed by Dionysos and make this god propitious by appeasing him with mystic initiations as well as other sacred performances. No man sets foot on the island, although the women themselves, sailing from it, have intercourse with the men and then return again... It is a custom of theirs, once a year, to unroof the temple and roof it again on the same day before sunset, each woman bringing her load to add to the roof; but the woman whose load falls from her arms is rent to pieces by the rest, and they carry the pieces round the temple and do not cease until their frenzy ceases."[117]

As has already been noted several times, animal sacrifice initially played a significant role in the cult of Dionysos. For example, his worship at one biennial festival on Crete involved the re-enactment of his death. The votaries worked themselves up into a frenzy until they were able to rip apart a live bull with their teeth. It seems very likely that this act was a sort of holy communion, in which the worshippers felt themselves to be eating the flesh and drinking the blood of their deity. Goats might also be ripped apart and consumed; doubtless this was for identical reasons.

There is also some evidence of human sacrifice to Dionysos; this is reported to have taken place at Chios and Tenedos. At Orchomenus in Boeotia, the culmination of the festival of *Agrionia*, which was dedicated to Dionysos *Agrionios* ('the wild'), was the pursuit and murder of a woman belonging to the royal family, recalling an occasion when several daughters of the king had been seized with a bacchic frenzy and had eaten a child.

Some scholars have suggested that the sacrifice of animals was a later substitute for offering a human; certainly, later at Tenedos the practice came to involve dressing up a new-born calf

117 Strabo, *Geography*, 4, 4, 6.

in boots whilst its mother was looked after like a woman in child-bed. Likewise, at Potniai in Boeotia, there was a temple dedicated to Dionysos *Aigobolos* (the 'goat-slayer'). The local legend was that once, when sacrifices were being offered to the god, the celebrants became so violently drunk that they actually killed the officiating priest. Immediately after the murder the citizens were visited by plague, to cure which the Delphic oracle said that they must sacrifice a boy in the bloom of youth. A few years afterwards, though, the god allowed a goat to be substituted as a victim in place of the boy.[118]

The more general practice may have been for sacrifice of live animals to have gradually been replaced. For example, at Kynathea in Arcadia a winter festival was held for Dionysos, at which men smeared with grease would try to seize a bull from a herd of cattle and then carry it to the sanctuary. As the geographer Pausanias observed, "this is the manner of their sacrifice."[119]

The point of all these rites was for the worshipper to become identified with the deity. The result is that "both votary and god are called Bacchus" in sources. The practices of so-called *omophagia* (eating of raw flesh) may also have been intended to echo Hera's consumption of the body of the body of baby Dionysos after he was murdered by the Titans.[120]

FESTIVALS OF DIONYSOS

There were two types of celebration of Dionysos in classical Greece. These were agricultural festivals, in which the god's role in fertility and fecundity were the focus, and the complex and private mystery rites (called *orgia*).

The state or public events were periods of licence, intoxication and of sacrifice. Overall, they were of four broad types: there

118 Aelian, *On Animals* 12, 34; Pausanias, *Description of Greece*, 9, 8, 2.
119 Pausanias, *Description of Greece*, 8, 19, 2.
120 W. Burkert, *Greek Religion*, 1985, 162.

were events associated with wine production; festivals involving dissolution and inversion; rustic feasts at which goats were sacrificed, and a few maritime events.

The Dionysia

The *Dionysia, Haloa,* and *Lenaia* were all agricultural festivals dedicated to Dionysos. The Rural or Lesser Dionysia was one of the oldest festivals held in honour of the god. It originated in Attica and celebrated the cultivation of vines (the second day of the feast was called *Askolia*, deriving its name from the word *askos,* meaning a wineskin; these were paraded – and danced upon – as part of the festival). The Rural Dionysia was held during the winter month of Poseidon (the time surrounding the winter solstice, modern December or January). The festival centred on a procession, during which participants carried phalluses, long loaves of bread, jars of water and wine and other offerings. The procession was followed by a series of dramatic performances and drama competitions, as well as drinking contests.

The City or Greater Dionysia took place in urban centres such as Athens and Eleusis. It was a later development, held three months after the Rural Dionysia, near to the spring equinox in about March or April. There was a procession led by participants carrying a wooden statue of Dionysos, to which bulls were sacrificed. Major dramatic competitions took place with important prizes for poets, dramatists and actors.

Haloa

Haloa was an annual harvest festival, giving thanks to the gods for the 'first fruits' of the year. It was celebrated principally at Eleusis in Attica and was dedicated to Demeter, goddess of crops, Poseidon, god of the seashore vegetation, and to Dionysos as god of the grape and of wine. The festival's name derives from the Greek word for a threshing floor, underlining its agrarian roots.

However, the inclusion of Dionysos in the celebrations had the effect of shifting the event later in the year to coincide with the grape rather than grain harvest.

Haloa was predominantly, if not exclusively, a women's festival, although our information about its ceremonies is scant. A very late source tells us that the women performed rituals involving "pits, snakes, pigs, and clay models of genitalia, all of which have a more or less marked sexual significance." These were performed as part of the sacred 'mysteries' and initiation ceremonies also took place.[121]

When *Haloa* was linked with Dionysos, a story grew up to explain this association. Dionysos was said to have presented an Attic shepherd called Icarius (Ikarios) with the gift of wine as a gesture of thanks for receiving his hospitality. However, when Icarius introduced his friends to the drink, they became intoxicated, thought he had poisoned them and killed him. Dionysos punished these shepherds by appearing to them in the form of a young woman, maddening them with sexual desire. However, as soon as she had aroused them, she disappeared, leaving the shepherds with erections that wouldn't abate until an oracle advised them to placate the god by dedicating clay models of genitals. Making these became a key custom of the festival. In addition, *Haloa* involved "lusty words" and activities, and the consumption of much wine and pornographic cakes. Women celebrated alone so that could enjoy freedom of speech – the priestesses apparently whispering rude words to the celebrants, who allowed themselves to make all sorts of coarse jokes and remarks.

Lenaia

The *Lenaia* was a less important Athenian festival that was held each year in January in honour of Dionysus *Lenaios* (the god of

121 M. Williamson, *The Sacred & Feminine in Ancient Greece*, 1998, 8.

the wine press). Its main feature was a dramatic competition. Once again, the rituals performed are not fully known, but it seems to have involved a torchlight nocturnal procession of singing maenads led by priests, ending in a sacrifice. The festival was an agrarian one, in origin, marking the pruning of the vines at the start of the year; symbolically, it represented the rebirth of the god.

Anthesteria

Anthesteria was an Athenian festival marking the start of spring and the maturation of the previous year's vintage. It lasted for three days, which were called *Pithoigia* (Jar-Opening), *Khoes* (Pouring) and *Khythroi* (Pots). On the first day of *Anthesteria*, wine jars were opened and the wine was offered to the god. On the second day, there was a solemn ritual for Dionysos, in which a ritual queen was married to the deity, possibly with some form of sexual intercourse taking place. This was followed by general festivities; people dressed up, often as members of Dionysos' entourage, visited friends and drank copious amounts of wine. The liberating aspect of Dionysos was manifested in the fact that slaves were permitted to participate in the festivities with households.

On the third and last day of *Anthesteria* food and drink was offered to the souls of the deceased. The dead were believed to rise from the underworld for the duration of the event and the female death spirits called the *keres* stalked the streets. These had to be banished when the festival ended by means of a ritual cry. The festivities and copious drinking continued on the third day, nonetheless.

BACCHIC MYSTERIES

The central religious rites of Dionysos are known as the Bacchic or Dionysian Mysteries. Evidence indicates that many sources and rituals typically considered to be part of the similar Orphic Mysteries (see later) actually belong to Dionysian ceremonies. These urban, cult-association based rites have to be distinguished from the public festivals, as well as from the all-female bacchanalian rites that took place in the hills and mountains outside towns and cities and which were described previously.

Initiation into the full mysteries seems to have been restricted in various ways. For instance, Plato, in *Phaedo,* stated that the "true worshippers [of Bacchus] are, in my opinion, none other than those who have practiced philosophy correctly." It may be that only women experienced the holy frenzy and were allowed to receive full initiation whilst men may only enjoyed limited participation, being allowed to join in some dances and to pay their homage to the god. Only initiates (*mystai*), it appears, was allowed to wear the fawn-skin – perhaps from an animal sacrificed at their initiation ceremony.[122]

These last statements notwithstanding, it has also been proposed that a man led the ceremonies as ritual specialist and initiator, for the reason that he played the role of the god himself. This priest seems to have been called the *boukolos,* the 'cow-herd,' reflecting the rural roots of the cult. In addition, as time passed, attendance at orgies is known to have got more mixed, although men's participation may have remained subject to limits – for example, only women ever became possessed.[123]

The mysteries were celebrated by groups in an imitation cave, another inheritance from the cult's rural origins. They would involve fire (for sacrifices and purifications), burning torches, and a chest containing the sacred cultic objects (such as phalli and winnowing fans – for which see 'Epithets' earlier). There were libations, dancing, singing and the declamation of ritual verses, as well as communal feasting and drinking.

---

122 *Phaedo*, 69c & d.

123 Euripides, *Bacchae*, 240 et seq; Kraemer, 'Ecstasy & Possession,' 70–72; Diodorus, *Historia*, 4.2.6.

The evidence suggests that there was some initiatory aspect to the Bacchic rites, in that they particularly marked a female's passage from child to adult, from a single to a married state. In addition, functions were divided between age groups, as Diodorus Siculus observed:

> "Bacchic bands of women gather, and it is lawful for the maidens to carry the thyrsos and to join in the frenzied revelry, crying out "Euai!" and honouring the god, while the matrons, forming in groups, offer sacrifices to the god and celebrate his mysteries and, in general, extol with hymns the presence of Dionysus, in this manner acting the part of the maenads who, as history records, were of old the companions of the god."[124]

The Bacchic mysteries thus served an important role in creating ritual traditions that marked transitional events in people's lives. These were often symbolised by a meeting with one of the gods responsible for death and change, such as Dionysos' mother Semele, who probably served a role related to initiation into the mysteries.

ORPHIC MYSTERIES

> "Pronouncing oracles from tall white tombs
> By the nymphs tended."
>
> (*Instructions to the Orphic Adept,* Robert Graves)

The story of Orpheus, musician son of the King of Thrace, is entwined with that of Dionysos. By some accounts, mortal Orpheus may have been an incarnation of the deity. He is also alleged to have been a seer and magician like the young god.

124 *Historia Biblioteca* 4.3.3.

Certainly, we know that, when Orpheus' lover, Eurydice, died, he went into Hades to recover her, thus sharing with the youthful Dionysos the association with resurrection and rebirth. However, Orpheus was not a deity. Rather, he was an ordinary man who worshipped the sun, or Apollo. Because of this, his fate was to be captured and dismembered as a heretic by some maenads when they came across him one day, performing a religious ceremony near to a shrine to Dionysos. In another version of the death of Orpheus, it was not his blasphemy but his refusal to have sex with the maenads that provoked their rage.

In the Orphic tradition, Dionysos performed the role of patron god connected with death and immortality. This was because the first incarnation of Dionysos, the son of Zeus and Persephone, had been dismembered by the Titans but was then reborn. He therefore symbolised the one who guides the process of reincarnation.

Because of the parallels, it has even been said that Orpheus invented the mysteries of Dionysos. It appears to be the case that the Orphic mysteries were a combination of the cult of Dionysos with other philosophical and religious ideas that entered Greece from the east. The principle Orphic idea was that man was a compound of divine and wicked nature and, as a result, the aim of the mystery was to enable the person to purge him or herself of the baser parts of the soul through rituals and by moral purity over a succession of reincarnations into a series of lifetimes. At the end of this extended process, the soul would have become fully divine and would have been freed from the cycle of death and rebirth. It's here that there was, perhaps, the most significant divergence from the cult of Dionysos. His rites were intended to be transcendental: through intoxication and possession – the "blessings of madness" – the worshipper could become united with the god there and then – the lifetimes of effort and spiritual evolution could be avoided. This immediate contact with the divine – this absorption of or into the divinity – remains the most attractive aspect of the bacchic rites. Some Dionysian adherents did, apparently, believe in rebirth into some sort of afterlife, but the sources are far from clear on the nature of this idea.[125]

It has been argued that the Orphic cult was a conscious attempt to reform and to 'tone-down' the Dionysian religion. This involved purifying and exalting it above its orgiastic roots, doing away with excess and making it calmer and more civilised and – as such – more suited to Greek culture and sensibilities. Any elements that were felt to be cruder or primitive were purged; the idea of intoxication was spiritualised, rather than being a literal state, and the deity was ennobled.[126]

WORSHIP AND FESTIVALS IN ROME

Dionysos, either under the Roman's preferred name of Bacchus (from Greek *Bakkhos*), or bearing an entirely Latin title, was nearly as actively worshipped in Italy as in Greece.

Liber and Importation to Rome

> "Help me, good Liber: and may another vine burden the elm, and the grapes be filled with the imprisoned juice, may the bacchae and the vigorous young satyrs be here, and their cries of inspiration not be silent, may the bones of Lycurgus the axe-bearer be crushed, and Pentheus."[127]

The mystery cult of Bacchus arrived in Rome from the Greek colonies of southern Italy or by way of Greek-influenced Etruria. It seems to have quickly become popular and well-organised throughout central and southern Italy and by around 200 BCE was established in the city of Rome on the Aventine hill, near

125 Pseudo-Apollodorus, *Bibliotheca Library and Epitome*, 1.3.2.

126 Guthrie, *Orpheus & Greek Religion*, 1993; P. McGinty, *Interpretation & Dionysos*, 2013, 84.

127 Ovid, *Tristia (Letters from Exile)*, 5.3.1.

where the Latin divinity *Liber Pater* (the Free Father) already had a state-sanctioned and popular temple.

Liber was the native Roman god of vines, wine, fertility, and prophecy. Increasingly, he was seen as being identical with Dionysos and shared his mythology. In fact, the two gods may have had a much more ancient link. The Mycenaean god Eleutheros shared the lineage and iconography of Dionysos while his name has the same meaning as *Liber*. The freedom these cults involved was not just the liberating sensation of drunkenness but also the licence that was generally permitted to individuals during festivals.

Bacchanalia

The bacchanals were the Latin equivalent of the private *orgia* celebrated in Greece. They seem to have shared a number of common elements: a large and leading role for women, the involvement of young men, an emphasis on sexuality and aggression, night time celebrations and, ultimately, as we shall see, official regulation.

The bacchanalia were unofficial, individually funded events. Like all ancient mystery cults, they were conducted in strict privacy and initiates were bound to secrecy. The result is that – as in Greece – very little is known of the actual rituals. The bacchanalia would appear to have incorporated both private and public elements; there were religious dramas performed in public and exclusive mystery rites conducted in private houses by acolytes and priests of the deity. The rituals are likely to have included the eating of raw flesh, often after pulling live animals apart. This practice served not only as a re-enactment of the infant death and rebirth of Bacchus, but also as a means by which Bacchic practitioners produced 'enthusiasm' and became united with the deity.

According to the Roman historian Titus Livy (who wrote nearly two hundred years after the events), the mysteries were originally restricted to women and held only three times a year during the daytime. However, they were gradually corrupted by Etruscan-Greek influence and became nocturnal events that were held five times a month and featured drinking and feasting. This drew an enthusiastic following of both women and men. As a result, the bacchanalia degenerated into drunken sexual free-for-alls at which inebriated and disinhibited men and women of all ages and classes mixed together, accompanied by shouting and the clashing of drums and cymbals. Livy described frenzied rites "full of lewdness," sexually violent initiations, immodesty, corruption and "the promiscuous matings of free men and women."[128]

Livy was something of a biased witness. He was inclined to a conservative stance on both morals and politics and, as such, he was a firm supporter of the Roman establishment, being friendly with members of the family of the Julii, most notably the Emperor Augustus and his nephew, the future Emperor Claudius. Livy saw the bacchanalia as "vile and alien rites," a violation of not only Roman laws but of traditional moral values. It was a false religion, a "whirlpool" that dragged people away from the worship of their ancestral gods. He disapproved too of private assemblies that had no established, rational, public purpose.

Livy attacked the cult because he felt it had encouraged the breakdown of strict social barriers. He did this by portraying it as a secretive, subversive and potentially revolutionary underground movement that was attracting thousands of "enthralled" adherents. The majority of these were women, whom he regarded as the primary source of the mischief, but with them were "men very like the women, debauched and debauchers, fanatical..." If effeminacy alone had been the result, it might have been tolerable, but Livy characterised the cult as the source of all lust, crime and fraud in the city. Worse still, as their numbers of cult members grew, they plotted moving from private offences to

128 Livy, *History of Rome*, Book 39, c.8–17.

the overthrow of the state: the cult and its rites were merely a cover for poisonings and other murders that paved the way for insurrection.

The practice of the Dionysian rites was reined in by the state in 186 BCE. The Senate issued an edict that, whilst it did not ban the bacchanalia, did impose strict controls on the Bacchic cult organisations. Prior senatorial approval had to be obtained for meetings, which only three women and two men could attend. Existing cult chapters were dismantled and men were forbidden from entering Bacchus' priesthood.

After this, it seems that Bacchus was deliberately conscripted into the official Roman pantheon as an aspect of *Liber Pater*, with his celebration being inserted into the existing festival of Liberalia. In Roman culture, Liber, Bacchus and Dionysos became virtually identical and in this sanctioned form their mystery cults persisted well into the early Imperial era. Even so, these reformed and officially approved rites probably bore little resemblance to the former crowded, ecstatic and uninhibited bacchanalia.

Livy – and possibly the Roman Senate as well – may have misunderstood the nature of the bacchanals, but they accurately sensed that the Dionysian cult stood for something different and potentially disruptive in Roman society. Rather than venerating the Latin gods in their temples, the rites offered individual devotees an immersive personal access to the deity. This ecstatic mysticism, engaged in several times a week, certainly had the capacity to alter perceptions and relationships. Fear of this unknown and unquantified potentiality to change social interactions may well have been what motivated the state's intervention.

Livy melodramatically exaggerated the immoral and scandalous nature of the rites for his own personal, social and political reasons, and the Senate probably used the matter as a way of reasserting control after a period of war, but Livy's account is the one that people recall. Part of Livy's description is worth reproducing for its sensationalist tone:

> "From the time that the rites were performed in common, men mingling with women and the freedom of darkness added, no form of crime, no sort of wrongdoing, was left untried. There were more lustful practices among men with one another than among women. If any of them were disinclined to endure abuse, or reluctant to commit crime, they were sacrificed as victims. To consider nothing wrong... was the highest form of religious devotion among them. Men, as if insane, with fanatical tossings of their bodies, would utter prophecies; matrons, in the dress of bacchantes and with dishevelled hair and carrying blazing torches, would run down to the Tiber, and plunging their torches in the water (because they contained live sulphur mixed with calcium) would bring them out still burning... Within the last two years it had been ordained that no one beyond the age of twenty years should be initiated: boys of such age were sought for as admitted both vice and corruption."[129]

It seems highly probable that the Bacchic rites *did* change as a result of the transition from Greece to Rome. They lost contact with their roots and meaning and, very possibly, became more hedonistic and ecstatic. Livy took this further and, of course, generations of scholars since have read about and remembered those drunken orgies and have repeated the accounts, helping to consolidate the orgiastic image in popular history. More recently, for instance, the HBO series *Rome* perpetuated the myth for modern audiences, featuring the smoking of cannabis and the suggestion of sexual excess. It just sounds more fun – and it highlights yet again the fascination that the prospect of liberation through ecstasy can exert upon us.

---

129 Livy, *History*, Book 39, c.13.

POST-CLASSICAL WORSHIP

The last known worshippers of the Greek and Roman gods were converted to the Christian faith before 1000 CE, although in some measure this was achieved by sleight of hand, preserving the pagan deities as saints- hence we have St. Dionysius, whose name has descended to us as St Denis, patron saint of France.

This displacement notwithstanding, there were several isolated instances of revived worship of Dionysos during the medieval and early modern periods. According to the chronicle of Lanercost Abbey in Cumbria, during Easter 1282 John the parish priest of Inverkeithing, near Edinburgh, revived the cult of Priapus and Father Bacchus. He "compelled" young girls to dance in circles. Then the priest led a dancing procession of local women, singing and dancing himself at the front, carrying a representation of a phallus on a pole and trying to stir up their lust with scandalous language. John's behaviour shocked respectable local people, but attempts to dissuade him were violently rebuffed.

Later that same year the congregation assembled for a formal ceremony of making penance. John wanted some parishioners to physically punish others for their confessed sins but his flock objected violently to this hypocritical imposition- and the priest was knifed to death.[130]

Much later, in the eighteenth century, interest in the classical gods began to revive amongst more educated and wealthy men and some even toyed with ideas of renewing their worship. So-called 'Hellfire Clubs' appeared across Britain and Ireland. Though activities varied between the clubs, some of them were highly paganised, and featured shrines and sacrifices. Dionysos was one of the most popular deities, alongside goddesses like Venus and Flora.

---

130 H. Maxwell, *The Chronicle of Lanercost, 1272–1346*. 1913, 29–30.

In 1820, a farmer called Ephraim Lyon founded the Church of Bacchus in Eastford, Connecticut – perhaps in response to the growing temperance movement. He declared himself its High Priest, the qualifying condition for this post being that he had to become seriously drunk several times each year. Lyon took it upon himself to add all the notorious local drunks to the list of church membership, by this unilateral means accumulating as many as one thousand members in his congregation. He called them 'zealots,' but some objected to their inclusion because of the implicit slur upon their reputations – and a few even physically threatened Lyon. Anyone who took a temperance vow was excommunicated, but he found many relapsed and could be restored to the flock. Lyon maintained that those who died as members would go to join the bacchanalian revels in their own special heaven.[131]

The Hellfire Clubs (like many of the period) were perhaps semi-serious about their paganism, whereas for John, vicar of Inverkeithing, it's much harder to reach any judgment. He seems to have acted out of conviction- given the drastic break it created with his position and vocation; perhaps it was some kind of personal revelation or breakdown, his sexual urges erupting irrepressibly. Whatever his reasons, it seems informative that it was through Dionysos that John (and the others mentioned) sought expression and liberation.

As for Ephraim Lyon, he seems pretty clearly to have been having fun. If nothing else, his church supplied him with a tongue in cheek justification for his own binge drinking. Nonetheless, his activity has some significance. Bacchus unquestionably was not unfamiliar to people and, whilst Lyon was constructing his elaborate joke in Connecticut, elsewhere in the English-speaking world a serious devotion to Dionysos was being revived, as we shall soon see.

---

131 R. Bayles, *History of Wyndham County, Connecticut*, 1889, 1039–40.

CONCLUSIONS

The Dionysian religion is transcendental – it's about communing directly with the god. The Orphic mysteries were concerned with paradise postponed; Dionysos promised heaven right now – he was "the best source of joy in life for mortals."[132]

The classical festivals held to honour the god illustrate many of the key elements of his worship. They retained, mostly, connections to their agricultural origins, but prominence was given to those aspects that represented the themes of ecstasy, liberation and renewal in the cult.

Dionysos is presented as a protector of those who do not belong to conventional society. He symbolises the chaotic, dangerous and unexpected, everything which escapes human reason and which can only be attributed to the unforeseeable action of the gods and fate. Moreover, he provides encouragement, because he met similar challenges in his own life and overcame them. He was seen as an outsider promoting a foreign cult, and he prevailed; he was murdered and dismembered – but he rose again.

Moreover, the cult of Dionysos recognises – and embraces – the dualities of existence. It's about ecstasy and horror, the fullness of life and its loss and destruction; about wild noise and empty silence. Dionysos offers both individual and communal inspiration.[133]

The frenzy of the rites has two meanings. There is, firstly, the personal communion with the deity. Secondly, though, there is a deliberate stepping outside of social roles and norms of conduct. We've seen many examples of this through the ancient history of the cult: women escaping their husband's control; the classes and sexes mixing in Rome; men dressing as women. These behaviours may have been labelled madness but, as Euripides suggested in *The Bacchae*, the whole experience may have given celebrants

132 Euripides, *Cyclops* 521.
133 P. McGinty, *Interpretation & Dionysos*, 2013, 167.

access to an awareness that it was those who became possessed who were truly sane whereas those who resisted the god were those in the wrong and so who would face harm.[134]

In their passage over the millennia into modern thought, many of the facets of the classical views of Dionysos have survived. He remains a god of inspiration and liberation. However, his agricultural and fertility aspects have, by and large, ceased to be of relevance whereas the elements of sex and sexuality in his cult have assumed far greater significance. In the second part of this book, we shall examine these modern perceptions of the god of wine and madness.

134 Euripides, *Bacchae*, 196–196.

PART TWO

Dionysos in Modern Culture

Over the last two centuries, Dionysos has re-emerged into western culture. This is because it has been recognised again that the deity is concerned with our attempts to define our authentic humanity. As the traditional Judaeo-Christian views of the world have come to be questioned or rejected, Dionysos has offered an alternative mode of thought and living. His ecstatic transcendence addresses our hunger for change and evolution. He satisfies our desires to break beyond the human sense experience of this world and to discover something more.[1]

Dionysos/Bacchus remains a god of the present; he is about enjoying now and not fretting about the unknown and largely unchangeable future, as Anglican priest Robert Herrick summarised surprisingly well in his *Lyric to Bacchus*:

> "While the milder fates consent,
> Let's enjoy our merriment:
> Drink, and dance, and pipe, and play;
> Kiss our dollies night and day:
> Crowned with clusters of the vine,
> Let us sit, and quaff our wine.
> Call on Bacchus, chant his praise;
> Shake the thyrse, and bite the bays:
> Rouse Anacreon from the dead,
> And return him drunk to bed:
> Sing o'er Horace, for ere long
> Death will come and mar the song:
> Then shall Wilson and Gotiere [contemporary musicians]
> Never sing or play more here."

1 P. McGinty, *Interpretation & Dionysos*, 1–4.

Dionysos in Modern Literature & the Arts

> "Everything,
> Everything,
> Anything that is of any use –
> Spring nymphs, Dionysus."[2]

Dionysos has remained an inspiration to artists, philosophers and writers into the modern era. He is not just a figure from classical history or art, either – he can be a lived reality. For instance, Belfast novelist Forrest Reid had experiences during the 1890s that had "nothing whatever to do with religion [but were] ... created by some power outside myself." One hot June day while he was a student, he was revising for exams in a field in Northern Ireland. Suddenly, he sensed the imminent arrival of Hermes, Dionysos, and 'hairy-shanked Pan-of-the-Goats' and had the compelling urge to make contact with some spiritual liberation that was simultaneously reaching out towards him. "For, though there was no wind, a little green leafy branch was snapped off from the bough above me, and fell to the ground at my hand. I drew my breath quickly; there was a drumming in my ears; I knew that the green woodland before me was going to split asunder, to swing back on either side like two great painted doors..." He hesitated, but the vision continued: "the tree was growing in my room, and I could feel the hot sunshine on my hands and body." This experience notwithstanding, Reid recorded that he preferred Pan and Hermes to Dionysos because he was repelled by the cruelty he perceived to be part of the worship of the latter – "The darker, more mystic element... the truly religious element,

2 *Einsturzende Neubaten*, 'Alles.'

doubtless, with its blood-sacrifices and ecstasy, mingled lust and madness..."[3]

Around the same time, the essayist Max Beerbohm claimed to subscribe to the belief that Vulcan, Mercury, Pan and Dionysus all still lived on – albeit humbly – and, he assured his readers, the author looked forward keenly to the day when they would rule again, just as they had in the past.[4]

In 1890 Celtic revivalist William Sharp (who wrote poetry as Fiona Macleod) told a correspondent that he was working on a "lyrical drama... called 'Bacchus in India'; my idea is to deal in a new – and I hope poetic way – with Dionysos as the Joy-Bringer, the God of Joyousness. In the first part there is the union of all the links between Man and the World he inhabits: Bacchus goes forth in joy, to give his serene message to all the world. The second part, 'The Return,' is wild disaster, and the bitterness of shame: though even there, and in the Epilogue, will sound the clarion of a fresh Return to Joy." This work was never completed, but it gives an interesting sense of the still-potent influence of the young god.[5]

As we shall see, the cult of Dionysos has fed the modern arts- and they in turn have fuelled the revival of the god's worship amongst modern audiences.

FRIEDERICH NIETZSCHE

In his first book, *The Birth of Tragedy from the Spirit of Music* (1872) – which was reissued in 1886 as *The Birth of Tragedy, or Hellenism and Pessimism* – the German philologist and philosopher Friedrich Nietzsche proposed that a tension between Apollonian and Dionysian aesthetic principles had underlain

---

3 Reid, *Apostate*, 1926, 158–9 & 210, and *Private Road*, 1940, 125 & 196–7.

4 Max Beerbohm, 'Hellas via Bradfield' in *Recreations and Reflections: Being Middles from the Saturday Review*, 1902, 146.

5 *William Sharp- A Memoir Compiled by his wife Elizabeth A. Sharp*, 1910, 171–172.

the development of Greek tragedy, with Dionysos representing what was unrestrained, chaotic and irrational, while Apollo represented the rational and ordered.

It is perfectly true to say that Greek myth contrasted Dionysos as a force of nature with the ethical and rational Apollo. Nevertheless, Nietzsche alone was responsible for this idea of a strict intellectual dichotomy and opposition between the Dionysian and the Apollonian elements in Greek drama. He went even further, too, claiming that life always involves a struggle between these two elements, each battling for control over human existence; each, however, holds the other in balance.

The first fifteen chapters of *The Birth of Tragedy* examined the nature of Greek tragic drama, which Nietzsche claimed was born when the Apollonian worldview met the Dionysian. The last ten chapters of the book then used the Greek model to understand the state of modern culture – both its decline and its possible rebirth. The tone of the text aims to be challenging and inspirational. Nietzsche repeatedly urged his readers to accept the culture of Dionysus again.

Firstly, Nietzsche described the state of Greek dramatic art before the influence of the visionary Dionysos. He alleged that it was naive, concerned only with appearances. As a result, audiences were never truly immersed in or united with the artistic performances, but remained always separated in quiet contemplation, and thereby shielded from the innate suffering of the world.

Then came Dionysos, whose ecstatic revels initially shocked Greek culture; yet, this madness brought the greatest blessings upon Greece and its civilisation. In the end, it was only through immersion in the Dionysian essence of primordial unity that redemption from the suffering of the world could truly be achieved. Through Dionysos, people realised that their existence was not limited to individual experiences alone, and, in this way, they found a route of escape from the fate of all men, which is death. The essence of Dionysos is eternal, so that anyone who connects with it will find a new source of life and hope. Turning from classical drama, Nietzsche thus showed Dionysos to be an uplifting alternative to the salvation offered by Christianity, which demands that people renounce life on earth altogether so that they may focus on a future salvation in heaven. By contrast, in order to be saved through Dionysos, the individual has to immerse him or herself in life now.[6]

In ancient Greece, Nietzsche argued, such access to Dionysian salvation had to come through the medium of a structured dramatic process in which Apollonian elements kept the chaos of Dionysos under control, preventing audiences being overwhelmed by ecstasy. He therefore emphasised that, in real tragic art, the elements of Dionysus and Apollo were inextricably entwined and counterpoised.

Nietzsche contended that the tragedy of ancient Greece had represented the highest form of art exactly because it was a mixture of both Apollonian and Dionysian elements, fused into a perfect whole that allowed audiences to experience the full spectrum of the human condition. The Dionysian aspects were to be found in the music of the chorus, while the Apollonian element was found in the dialogue, which gave a concrete meaning that balanced the Dionysian symbolism. As words could never hope to delve into the depths of the Dionysian essence, choral music was essential, allowing participants to rise beyond consciousness and experience a connection with the primordial unity. In summary, the Apollonian spirit was able to give form to the Dionysian abstraction. The two were artistically woven together and the spectator became healthy through direct experience of the Dionysian within the protective spirit-of-tragedy on the Apollonian stage.

For Nietzsche, Dionysos was "an artist in both dreams and ecstasies," whilst the core nature of Dionysian rites was a

6 *Birth of Tragedy*, 7–8.

"strenuous becoming [and] grown self-consciousness." The cult helped followers to "strive after creation, after the voluptuousness of wilful creation." Dionysian madness brought visions and hallucinations, it brought joy; he compared it to drunkenness – it was a "mystical self-abnegation," a "complete self-forgetfulness."[7]

> "We are really- for brief moments- Primordial Being itself, and feel its indomitable desire for being and joy in existence; the struggle, the pain, the destruction of phenomena, now appear to us as something necessary, considering the surplus of innumerable forms of existence which throng and push one another into life, considering the exuberant fertility of the universal will. We are pierced by the maddening sting of these pains at the very moment when we have become, as it were, one with the immeasurable primordial joy in existence, and when we anticipate, in Dionysian ecstasy, the indestructibility and eternity of this joy. In spite of fear and pity, we are the happy living beings, not as individuals, but as the *one* living being, with whose procreative joy we are blended."[8]

Nietzsche felt that this fully developed classical Athenian tragedy was an art form that transcended the pessimism and nihilism of a fundamentally meaningless world. The Greek spectators, by looking into the abyss of human suffering and affirming it, were then able passionately and joyously to affirm the meaning of their own existence. They knew themselves to be infinitely more than insignificant individuals living brief lives, and they found self-affirmation not in promises of another life in a world to come, but in the terror and ecstasy of their current lives as they were dramatised and celebrated in the tragedies. This view of the Greeks was so alien to the spirit of his own time and to the ideals of its scholarship that it drew numerous attacks and

7 Nietzsche, *Birth of Tragedy*, 1886, xix, 7, 28–29.
8 *Birth of Tragedy*, 111, 128–129 & 160.

blighted Nietzsche's entire academic career (and, sadly, *The Birth of Tragedy* was his first book).

However, Nietzsche believed that this perfect fusion of opposites within Greek drama did not last. Euripides and Socrates had excluded Dionysos from the dramatic arts, he alleged. Euripides scaled back the musical part, the role of the chorus, and made plays more naturalistic and realistic; Socrates put the emphasis upon rationality. The effect of the loss of this "highest musical orgasm" was to exclude audiences from truly participating in or becoming transported by drama.[9]

Music had permitted a spectator to "abandon herself unhesitatingly to an orgiastic feeling of freedom." The reduction of the musical element had the effect of "destroying the essence of tragedy, which can be explained only as a manifestation and illustration of Dionysian states, as the visible symbolisation of music, as the dream-world of Dionysian ecstasy." Dionysian art, in Nietzsche's view, sought to convince participants of the "eternal joy of existence;" this state is transient, and will assuredly come to "a sorrowful end" – but that is in the nature of things.

The contemporary problem, Nietzsche therefore thought, was how the highest Greek dramatic achievement could be re-attained – how the "blissful" and "sublime" ecstasy that Dionysos offered could be recovered. How could audiences experience and understand the Dionysian side of life without destroying the obvious values of the Apollonian side? It was not healthy for an individual, or for a whole society, to become entirely absorbed in the rule of one or the other; the soundest and healthiest position was to be able to experience both, Nietzsche believed.

In the latter part of his book, Nietzsche explored the modern ramifications of the shift that had taken place in Greek drama. He argued that society was living in the final stages of this failed Greek culture of rationality. Science could not explain the mysteries of the universe, so that the time was ripe for a rebirth of

9 *Birth of Tragedy*, 159.

the more balanced Dionysian perception. Nietzsche saw German music, particularly that of Richard Wagner, as the beginning of this transformation.

In Nietzsche's 1886 work *Beyond Good and Evil*, and subsequently in *The Twilight of the Idols*, and *The Antichrist*, Dionysos is conceived as the embodiment of life's vitality and exuberance whose aesthetic nature is opposed to the sterile morality of Christianity and its focus on a 'better life' in another world. In 1888, in *Ecce Homo*, Nietzsche returned to the attack. He proposed Dionysian suffering as the root of the whole of Greek art and again condemned Socrates' rationality as a dangerous force that had undermined life.[10]

This concept of a rivalry or opposition between Dionysos and Apollo has been characterised as a modern myth, as it is the invention of thinkers like Nietzsche and Johann Joachim Winckelmann and is not found in classical sources. However, the acceptance, popularity and influence of this perspective in Western culture have been very considerable. For instance, in his books *The Hellenic Religion of the Suffering God* (1904), and *Dionysos and Early Dionysianism* (1923), the Russian symbolist poet Vyacheslav Ivanov elaborated Nietzsche's theory of the cultural role of Dionysos, tracing the origins of literature, and tragedy in particular, to ancient Dionysian mysteries. Ivanov believed that Dionysos' suffering "was the distinctive feature of the cult" just as Christ's suffering is central to Christianity. He saw Dionysos as an earlier manifestation of Jesus and felt that the cult could be a route to universal brotherhood. Ivanov was a disciple of what he called 'mystical anarchism' and was interested generally in spiritualism, the occult and the work of Rudolf Steiner. He also founded a Bacchic commune and believing himself to be a mortal incarnation of Dionysos, calling the god 'The Black Sun.' He was not alone in this: one evening in May 1905 in the St Petersburg home of the poet Nicolai Minsky, a

10 *Birth of Tragedy*, 10–11.

group of Symbolists met to perform a rite which tried to imitate the Mysteries of Dionysos and induce ecstasy in the participants. It involved drinking a woman's blood and caused such a scandal that Minsky had to leave Russia. Nonetheless, such spiritual experiments reflected Ivanov's preoccupation with the perceived gulf between the spiritual values of antiquity and the materialism and barrenness of contemporary society, and – like Nietzsche – with the contrast between the ecstatic cult of Dionysos and the joyless rigidity of institutionalized religion. Ivanov envisaged a kind of participative theatre which would allow the audience to get involved in what would constitute a sacred rite.

Whilst we do not have to sympathise with – or even necessarily fully grasp – Nietzsche's ideas, it is important to recognise how influential his concept has been. It has had an impact on numerous subsequent thinkers, amongst them the British occultist and magician Aleister Crowley (1875–1947).

ALEISTER CROWLEY

In the magical and quasi-religious system of *Thelema* (a Greek word meaning 'divine will'), which Aleister Crowley expounded in his first major work *The Book of the Law* (1909) – and which formed the basis for the neo-religious movement he founded called the *Church of Thelema* – the god Dionysus occupied a central (but not exclusive) position, a magical role that one writer has summarised in these terms: "The way of Pan and Bacchus is the preferred mode of being." A small initial example of the significance of Dionysos in Crowley's practice is the so-called 'Vir' gesture he frequently used. This may be familiar from the well-known 1910 photograph of 'the Beast' wearing his 'tea-cosy' magician's hat (properly, his head-dress of Horus), staring intently at the camera, both hands raised on either side of his head, fists clenched and thumbs protruding. This symbolised the horns of a ram and, hence, Pan/Bacchus. Bacchus stood for action and for the spiritual phallus.[11]

The doctrines of *Thelema* were blended from ideas borrowed freely from astrology, yoga, alchemy, Hinduism, Taoism, Qabalah, the I Ching, Gnosticism, Christianity, Rosicrucianism and the ancient religions of Greece and Egypt. Crowley was highly eclectic in the traditions from which he drew his inspiration, although Buddhist theories and Egyptian deities were probably most significant. Nonetheless, the importance of the Dionysos in this scheme was affirmed in his essay *The Book of Thoth: A Short Essay on the Tarot of the Egyptians*, in which Crowley treated him as the primary deity. He also identified the young god with Pan (as we have just seen), Pan with the Devil, and the Devil with himself. Crowley, it can't be ignored, had a high regard for his own importance, hence the titles he granted himself- which included the Great Beast 666, Baphomet and Master Therion. Still, the ultimate aim, in all his work, was to rediscover and re-awaken the great nature gods of the pagan past.[12]

Referring to Friedrich Nietzsche's theories, Crowley saw Dionysos as being Christ- one of many examples of a reborn or resurrected god to be found in the great mystery cults throughout religious history. In fact, Crowley went so far as to regard the story of Jesus' life to be "only a corruption and perversion of other stories." He recognised that the Dionysian cult of death and rebirth was fundamentally concerned with the processes of the natural world and that the young god has "identity with the course of Nature – its madness, its prodigality, its intoxication, its joy and, above all, its sublime persistence through the

11 D. Webb, *Overthrowing the Old Gods – Aleister Crowley & the Book of the Law*, 2013; R. Orpheus, *The Grimoire of Aleister Crowley*, 2019, 86, 100 & 131. Equally, during his Paris working in January 1914, Crowley made a statue of Hermes out of wax that resembled a penis-shaped wand (Booth, *Magick Life*, 313).

12 'The Book of Thoth' in *The Equinox*, volume III, number 5, March 1944; Fuller, *The Star in the West*, 323.

cycles of Life and Death..." Crowley believed that nature could be a source of tragedy and sorrow unless one approached it correctly. Confronted with such a harsh reality, he advised that the aspiring magician "should consider if there is not some deity who expressed this cycle [of life and death] and yet whose nature is joy. He will find what he requires in Dionysus..." In fact, Bacchus could become the magician's 'Holy Guardian Angel,' a manifestation of his higher self, that part of ourselves that is in touch with the infinite universal spirit, and would then protect and guide him, magically and spiritually.[13]

Nietzsche's work appears to have influenced Crowley in more than one way. Captain (later General) John Frederick Charles Fuller was one of the Beast's earliest supporters and in 1906 wrote a fulsome endorsement of his hero – *The Star in the West; a Critical Essay Upon the Works of Aleister Crowley*. Fuller characterised Crowley as "more than a new-born Dionysus; he is more than a Blake, a Rabelais or a Heine; he stands before us as some priest of Apollo, hovering 'twixt the misty blue of the heavens and the more certain purple of the vast waters of the deep." As such, Crowley's mission would appear to have been to reunite the Dionysian and Apollonian that had been sundered by Euripides and Socrates. A 'New Aeon of Horus' was predicted, which would involve a break with existing civilisation and a radical change in the prevailing moral sanctions. Crowley saw himself at the forefront of this "Equinox of the Gods;" he was to be the vehicle by which the "word of the Aeon" would be conveyed, with effects comparable to "The Cult of the Dying God introduced by Dionysus [which] destroyed Roman virtue and smashed Roman culture."[14]

---

13 Crowley, *The Book of Lies*, c.7, 29; J. Symonds & K. Grant (editors), *The Confessions of Aleister Crowley*, 1988, 720 & 795; Crowley, *Magick in Theory & Practice*, 1976, 12 & 263.

14 Fuller, *Star in the West*, 194; *Confessions*, 404.

The Nature of Magic

It is important here to stress the difference between Crowley's approach to and relationship with Dionysos and that of every other individual discussed in this book. The cult of the god was, and is, concerned with his worship and with attempts by devotees to achieve union with divinity. Crowley perceived the ancient deities quite differently.

Crowley was quite explicit about his aims. Magic, he said, is "the Science and Art of causing Change to occur in conformity with Will." He elaborated this statement by explaining that humans' "spiritual consciousness acts through the will and its instruments upon material objects, in order to produce changes which will result in the establishment of the new conditions which we wish." The gods of ancient Egypt and Greece are, therefore, not so much praised and adored as used – their powers are summoned by magicians to assist in the realisation of their purposes, rather than for the revelation of any expression of the divine will. Crowley's aim was always self-assertion, not self-effacement.[15]

Invoking the God

The young deity could be ritually and magically invoked in a number of ways. He could simply be called upon for aid, as happened when Crowley was writing the *Book of Lies* in 1913. He described the purpose of the book as being "to expound some profound magical dogma in an epigrammatic and sometimes humorous form." Crowley wrote chapters daily at lunch or dinner with the help of the god, he recalled, and, if he encountered difficulties, he would invoke the deity with "particular fervour." Elsewhere, Crowley claimed that "My muse is the daughter of Hermes and the mistress of Dionysus."[16]

15 See, for example, M. Booth, *A Magick Life – A Biography of Aleister Crowley*, 2000, 82.

16 *Book of Lies*, 5; *Confessions*, 227 & 409.

Another method of invocation was to seek to imitate or recreate the bacchanals of the classical Greeks. Crowley was acutely aware of the power of this approach, as he stated in *Magick*:

> "The third method of [invoking a deity] is the Dramatic, perhaps the most attractive of all; certainly, it is so to the artist's temperament for it appeals to his imagination through his aesthetic sense. Its disadvantage lies in the difficulty of its performance by a single person. But it has the sanction of the highest antiquity and is probably the most useful for the foundation of religion... The *Bacchae* of Euripides is a magnificent example of such a ritual..."

Crowley continued by outlining what might be hoped to be achieved through such a strategy. "The magician who wishes to invoke Bacchus by this method must therefore arrange a ceremony in which he takes the part of Bacchus, undergoes all his trials and emerges triumphant beyond death." He cautioned his readers on one particular point of interpretation here: the aim of passing beyond death was not personal immortality, but absorption into – or at least contact with – the universal spirit. If Crowley is correct on this point, then we may need to revise our understanding of what initiates into the Bacchic mysteries understood by 'afterlife' (see Part One).[17]

What is evident is that Crowley appreciated the value of the group experience in contacting Dionysos – that ecstasy was more easily achieved as part of a shared and mutually supporting and stimulating ceremony. Furthermore, despite the fact (as we shall soon see) that he wrote a number of hymns in praise of the god, Crowley came to see that dramatic invocation along the lines of Euripides' *Bacchae* might be a more effective method. Upon reflection, he admitted that:

17 Crowley, *Magick*, c.1.

> "By commemorating the story of the god, one might identify oneself with him and thus constitute a subtler, stronger and more complete invocation of him than by direct address. I might even go as far as to say that the form of the latter implies the consciousness of duality and therefore tends to inhibit identification."[18]

The bacchanalian means of invoking the god employed what Crowley termed the 'method of Dionysus.' With the help of self-transforming ecstasies and other techniques (such as the use of intoxicants and diverse sexual practices) the adept of *Thelema* was to be placed in states that unravelled his higher-self. Crowley's modern rituals for evoking Dionysos were set out in the book *Orpheus, A Lyrical Legend* (1905) and in the essay 'Energised Enthusiasm. A Note on Theurgy' that was published in *The Equinox* in 1913. Interestingly, though, he ended his discussion of energised enthusiasm with a description of a ritual he had once attended at a secluded chapel, possibly in France, along with a two dozen or so other initiates. Crowley depicted a ceremony involving sex, drugs and incense, which had induced a feeling of ecstasy in its participants. However, his conclusion was that "the obvious practical step to take is to restore Bacchus, Aphrodite and Apollo to their proper place. They should *not* be open to everyone and manhood should be the reward of ordeal and initiation..." He felt that individuals ought to work in secret on the "master-methods of aiding the soul to its genial orgasm."[19]

For Crowley, Dionysos was a powerful being whom it was beneficial to invoke in the course of rituals and ceremonies. For example, in the 'Proclamation of the Beast 666' he was called upon – "Hermes to hear, Dionysus to touch, Pan to behold." In the 'Office of the Collects which are Eleven in Number' he was named

18 Crowley, *Confessions*, 273.

19 *Energised Enthusiasm*, IX.

by the Mage in typically eclectic fashion, grouped in a mass alongside figures such as Lao Tse, Siddartha, Krishna, Moses, Mohammed, Priapus, Orpheus and Heracles.[20]

In imitation of the ancient models, Crowley consciously incorporated poetry, music and dance into the rites and workings he devised, which were developed through practical trial and error. What was found to work was codified in scripted ceremonies. He constantly strove to create a 'Dionysian' atmosphere at his rites, believing that "All frenzy is sacred to Dionysus." Hymns were sung to the deity, with celebrants in one instance calling on Bacchus to ride out of the east "on the Ass of Priapus," "Come in thy name, O Dionysus – that maidens may be mated to godhead!" As one authority has observed, Crowley's "worship of Dionysus was anything but solemn." Sometimes, admittedly, the atmosphere might be inhibited by the reality of the rite itself. For instance, on one occasion in late 1922, Crowley performed his dance of Dionysian frenzy for Betty May, a former prostitute and model, who was visiting the Abbey of Thelema in Sicily. She found it impressive – but funny; Crowley, of course, would have been approaching fifty, balding and increasingly overweight. In his *Confessions,* though, the magician recorded that he saw himself as the "Young Dionysus… I always feel myself as about eighteen or twenty."[21]

Nonetheless, as the bacchantes before him had discovered, dance could be a powerful means of generating communal ecstasy. In his lyrical legend of *Orpheus,* Crowley depicted its potency: "blinded by some Panic dust/By Dionysian din/ Deafened, aroused the laughing lust/To fling my body in." The maenads in the poem "weave/Dances to the mighty mother

20 L.M. Duquette, *Magick of Aleister Crowley – Handbook of Rituals of Thelema*, 2003, 20, 145 & 224.

21 Booth, *Magick Life*, 286; R. Orpheus, *Grimoire*, 104; C. Wilson, *Aleister Crowley – The Nature of the Beast*, 2003; Crowley, *Magick in Theory & Practice*, 1976, 263; *Confessions*, 116.

[Semele]!/Bacchanal to Bacchus cleave! Wave his narthex wand and leave/Earthy joys to earth to smother!"[22]

Sex Magick

> "The orgies of Bacchus and Pan are no less sacramental than the masses of Jesus."[23]

For Crowley, all aspects of sex were sacramental. He saw sexual activity as creative and ecstatic, an energy that could be channelled into magickal work so long as individual emotions and sentiment were not permitted to intrude.

Dionysos was particularly central to Crowley's workings in his 'Ceremony of Enthusiasm.' This was concerned with the frenzies inspired by three Greek gods, Dionysos, Aphrodite and Apollo- or wine, women and song. Apollo was the source of prophetic frenzy, which Crowley sought to stimulate through the music of voice, violin and drums. Aphrodite was the source of erotic frenzy, which he strove to arouse through his 'sexual method' or 'sex magick.' Caution has to be exercised in these workings though, as it is all too easy to become intoxicated, rather than inspired, and to be overcome by mere carnal lust rather than focussed upon the magical goals of the process. Crowley knew this from experience: in his diary for April 16th 1916, he recorded that a sex magic session with his then lover, Alice Ethel Coomaraswamy, had gone rather too well – "This operation is the most magnificent in all ways since I can remember. The Orgasm was such as to have completely drowned the memory of the Object." Properly harnessed, though, sexual energy could be used to transform a willed objective into reality.[24]

---

22 Crowley, *Orpheus*, 86 & 173. *Narthex* denotes the plant *Ferula narthex*, a wild fennel often identified with asafoetida.

23 Crowley, *Magick in Theory & Practice*, 338.

24 F. King, *The Magical World of Aleister Crowley*, 1978, 98; T. Churton, *Aleister Crowley- The Biography*, 2011, 230–231; Booth, *Magick Life*, 333.

As has been seen, expressions of sexuality were never far from the worship of Dionysos and, in the Roman bacchanalia and the Bacchic rites, sex appears to have been incorporated as a key element of celebration and initiation. Crowley identified the sex instinct as being identical to or synonymous with genius, or divinity, and, accordingly, sexual activities were integrated into his magical work – what he termed his 'method of Aphrodite.' For example, vigorous bouts of sex with male or female partners could release and combine energies and thereby facilitate divine communications. Rather as, in the ancient world, a priest or senior initiate of the cult may have assumed the role of the god and copulated with devotees, so too – it seems – was the practice during Crowley's workings. He recorded one ceremony when an unspecified god "came to us in human form… and remained with us… for the best part of an hour, only vanishing when we were physically exhausted by the ecstasy of intimate contact with his divine person." The twenty-three-year-old American Cecil Frederick Russell joined the Abbey of Thelema on Sicily in 1920 and was christened Iacchaion – after Iacchus, another name for Dionysos, which Crowley sometimes used for the god. Neophite Russell was expected to contribute a "Dionysian sexual ecstasy to worship," but in the event didn't live up to the Beast's hopes. What these may have involved might be inferred from Crowley's response to a person who had written to him, asking to be allowed to serve as a slave at the Abbey – "Come to me, that I may trample you underfoot and press out wine for the Lord Dionysus," he replied. The male and female secretions generated during bouts of magically inspired intercourse could (if you wished) be consumed as a sacrament, having been mixed together whilst invoking Bacchus, Aphrodite and Apollo.[25]

Lastly, Dionysos was contacted through the process that Crowley termed 'energised enthusiasm.' He believed that sexual

25 L. Sutin, *Do What Thou Wilt*, 2014, 288; King, *Magical World*, 138; Crowley, *Magick*, 263.

pleasure is connected to the same divine ecstasy that is achieved through such spiritual practices as meditation; it links us to the deepest parts of ourselves, which partake of the universal spirit. Accordingly, if used with care, sex could assist adepts to enhance their magical potential. Sex- used wisely- could therefore be a divine tool. Contrasting Crowley's techniques to the practices of the bacchantes of the ancient world, we might propose that they saw sexual ecstasy as the goal, whereas for him it represented more of a medium by which to accomplish his goals.[26]

Ecstasies

"Our ancient ecstasy, do you recall?"[27]

Rather than attaining ecstasy through the manic frenzy of the maenads, Crowley relied primarily upon alcohol and peyote, having experimented with drugs from about 1907 onwards, trying opium, cocaine, ether gas, ethyl alcohol, marijuana and calomel (mercury chloride). In 1904, Crowley had had a vision in which he had been advised to "take wine and strange drugs... They shall not harm ye at all." He respected this throughout his life and, guided by the sexologist Havelock Ellis, found that drops of peyote tincture taken in a glass of cold water and combined with sex could lead to intense spiritual experiences. Crowley, in turn, was alleged to have introduced Aldous Huxley to the mind-expanding properties of some drugs.[28]

Drug taking was integrated into many of Crowley's rituals. For example, in August 1910 he performed a 'Rite of Artemis' in public at the offices of the magazine *Equinox – The Review of Scientific Illuminism,* which were at 124, Victoria Street, London. In the

26 Churton, *Aleister Crowley*, 129, 138–9 & 255; Booth, *Magick Life*, 306 & 313–316.

27 Paul Verlaine, *Colloque Sentimental.*

28 Bogdan & Starr, *Aleister Crowley and Western Esotericism*, 2012; Crowley, *The Book of the Law*, II, 22.

course of this performance, the celebrants and audience drank several 'libations,' which seem to have been what Crowley called an 'elixir' combining anahalonium or mescal buttons, opium, herbs, fruit juice and alcohol. Attendees were *not* told what this "pleasant smelling drink" contained. His stated intention was to create a bacchic exuberance without the risk of getting people drunk on wine. He may have succeeded; apparently, the effects of the 'libation' lasted for up to one week.[29]

The August event had gone so well that it was decided to repeat the rites at a larger venue. Over seven weeks in October and November 1910, Crowley, with the help of Victor Neuberg as dancer- performing the "dance of Syrinx and Pan in honour of our lady Artemis" – and his lover Leila Waddell as musician, publicly celebrated the 'Rites of Eleusis' at the Caxton Hall in Westminster, London. The hall's capacity was one hundred and nearly full houses attended each performance, paying a hefty and ambitious £5 (£400 today) for admission (Crowley's fortune was beginning to run out by this stage). They experienced the same potent mix of music, costumes, props, recitation, incense, lighting and movement that had been so impressive in August.

In advance publicity for the ceremony, Crowley declared "We are the poets! We are the children of the wood and stream, of mist and mountain, of sun and wind! We are the Greeks! And to us the rites of Eleusis should open the doors to Heaven and we shall enter in and see God face to face." He told *The Sketch* (in an interview that was also reproduced in his publicity) that all the gods are "barren of hope until the spirit of the Infinite All, great Pan, tears asunder the veil and displays the hope of humanity, the Crowned Child of the Future. All this is symbolised in the holy rites which we have recovered from the darkness of history, and now in the fullness of time disclose that the world may be redeemed." Crowley announced that his adepts would "dance in the moonlight before Dionysus, and delight under the stars with

29 R. Kaczynski, *Perdurabo*, 2010, 218–219.

Aphrodite; yet they shall also dwell beyond all these things in the unchanged Heaven – Here and Now."

Over each of the seven weeks of the performance, a dedicated rite was celebrated for each of the different classical gods related to the days of the week, these being Saturn, Jupiter, Mars, Sol, Venus, Mercury and Luna. The aim was to generate "a carefully selected ecstasy" for each deity. Crowley sketched some of these in advance, although for the ecstasy to be expected for Venus, he asked "why labour the obvious?" something which doubtless excited his potential audiences.[30]

Within these rites other gods were prominent as well; for example, Isis was central to the rite of Venus, Jupiter manifested as Iacchus and Pan featured in the rite of Luna. Pan was especially important, being the "Holy Spirit of Matter, from which union [with Artemis] springs humanity." It appears, too, that certain drugs were linked to certain deities; for example, peyote was associated with Mercury. In addition to the drugs, the rituals involved poetry, most prominently the work of Algernon Charles Swinburne – a favourite of Crowley's – which featured in nearly all of the rites (see later). Alongside Swinburne's *Atalanta in Corydon* and *Garden of Proserpine,* Verlaine's *Colloque Sentimental* and James Thomson's *City of Dreadful Night* were recited.[31]

The ultimate purpose of the rites, Crowley recorded, was "the attaining of religious ecstasy by means of Ceremonial Magic." This ecstatic state would enable an individual to contact their Guardian Angel and thereby help to usher in the new aeon in human development. The practical risk, though, as Crowley himself discovered, was that "the hashish enthusiasm surged up against the ritual enthusiasm; so, I hardly know which phenomena to attribute to which."[32]

30 *The Bystander*, October 12th & November 23rd 1910.

31 Crowley, *The Rites of Eleusis*, 1911, 1 & 5–8; *The Sketch*, Aug. 24th & Oct. 26th 1910; *Bystander* Nov. 23rd 1910; Booth, *Magick Life*, 343.

32 Churton, *Aleister Crowley*, 7; Booth, *A Magick Life*, 241

Poetry

Some further sense of the processes Crowley used – and what he hoped to achieve – may be derived from examining a few of his poems. Readers should be warned that the mage had a high opinion of his verse: he once remarked, for example, on the "strange coincidence that one small county should have given England her two greatest poets – one must not forget Shakespeare." (The other bard referred to was Crowley himself, of course, born in Leamington Spa, Warwickshire, twelve miles from Stratford). However, he felt that many people would find his work hard going because of his intense passion, profound introspection and the obscure allusions, which demand serious study fully to understand them.[33]

Crowley's verse *Dionysus* is a hymn to the young god, seeing him as the motive power of nature, the bringer of physical and spiritual communion. This is, perhaps, a rather more traditional view than that expressed in his actual magical workings.

> "I bring ye wine from above,
> From the vats of the storied sun;
> For every one of ye love,
> And life for everyone.
>
> Ye shall dance on hill and level;
> Ye shall sing in hollows and height
> In the festal mystical revel,
> The rapturous Bacchanal rite!"

The god will help reveal things as they actually are: lifting "the mask of matter" and opening the heart so that individuals may realise that, at their core, they are Pan. The purpose of this drinking and dancing is to achieve union: "We are wed, we are

33 Crowley, *Confessions*, 35 & 227.

wild, we are one!" It will be apparent that, for Crowley, the distinction between Dionysos and Pan was minimal – they both represent the vital natural force.

The song of Dionysos was written as a part of *Orpheus – A Lyrical Legend* (1905). This work also includes a chorus of maenads who call on the god "Give me to drink! Hail, child of Semele!" He then appears "with serpent hair/And limbs divinely fair... leap[ing] forth to nectar air!" The impassioned women beseech him "Be close, be quick, be near/Whispering enchanted words in every curving ear! Oh, Dionysus, start/As the Apollonian dart! Bury thy horned head in every bleeding heart." Agave, queen of Thebes, addresses him as "lord of life and joy/ In whom we may perceive a subtle world/ Hidden beneath this masquerade of things."

A sonnet written by Crowley, and which was inspired by Rodin's bust of the poet W.E. Henley, imagined being in a woodland grove "Rich with Bacchus' frenzy and his wine's/ Atonement for the infinite woes of man/And here his mighty and reverend priest/Bade me good cheer, an eager acolyte/Poured the high wine/unveiled the magic feast..."

Crowley's 1919 *Hymn to Pan* pursued the connection, or intersection, between the two divine beings- and between the divine and the mortal (male) worshipper. Crowley places himself in the role of maenad (or perhaps Ariadne) and is overwhelmed by an ecstasy of erotic passion, singing in terms that echo Philodamus' *Paean to Dionysos.* Crowley modestly assessed the *Hymn* as "the most powerful enchantment ever written" and it undeniably has a distinct energy in its rhythm and insistent pulse of alliteration and consonance.[34]

"Thrill with lissome lust of the light,
O man! My man!
Come careering out of the night

34 Crowley, *Confessions*, 20 & 841.

Of Pan! Io Pan!...
Come over the sea
From Sicily and from Arcady!
Roaming as Bacchus, with fauns and pards
And nymphs and satyrs for thy guards,
On a milk-white ass, come over the sea
To me, to me!
Come... wash thy white thigh, beautiful god,
In the moon of the woods, on the marble mount,
The dimpled dawn of the amber fount!
Dip the purple of passionate prayer
In the crimson shrine, the scarlet snare,
The soul that startles in eyes of blue
To watch thy wantonness weeping through
The tangled grove, the gnarled bole,
Of the living tree that is spirit and soul
And body and brain – come over the sea,
(Io Pan! Io Pan!)
Devil or god, to me, to me...
Come with trumpets sounding shrill
Over the hill!
Come with drums, low muttering,
From the spring!
Come with flute and come with pipe!
Am I not ripe?...
Come, oh come!
I am numb
With the lonely lust of devildom.
Thrust the sword through the galling fetter,
All-devourer, all-begetter;
Give me the sign of the Open Eye,
And the token erect of thorny thigh,
And the word of madness and mystery...
I am a man:

Do as thou wilt, as a great god can…
I am awake
In the grip of the snake.
The eagle slashes with beak and claw;
The gods withdraw:
The great beasts come. Io Pan! I am borne
To death on the horn
Of the Unicorn …
I am thy mate, I am thy man,
Goat of thy flock, I am gold, I am god,
Flesh to thy bone, flower to thy rod.
With hoofs of steel, I race on the rocks
Through solstice stubborn to equinox.
And I rave; and I rape and I rip and I rend
Everlasting, world without end,
Mannikin, maiden, maenad, man,
In the might of Pan…"

As will be apparent, Crowley's conception of the Greek divinities was intensely sensual and physical. He identified himself with them and partook of their passions, using powerful homoerotic imagery.

Lastly, Crowley's verse *Pan to Artemis* was written in 1911 to be recited by Leila Waddell during the Rites of Eleusis after she had been enthroned as a representative of the goddess, invoking lunar influence. In the poem, Crowley addressed Artemis as the "Uncharmable charmer/Of Bacchus and Mars" and imagined a "night of delight" with her such as those gods enjoyed. It is a "secret communion" or a "mystical union/Of fairy and faun." In fact, Crowley typically and immodestly saw himself as having sexual powers that Bacchus and other deities lacked: "No Godhead could charm her/But manhood awoke."

Sexuality

What also comes out strongly from Crowley's poems is his deep concern with the dual sexual nature (*diphues*) of Dionysos. He was also fascinated by Zeus in his hermaphrodite form, called *Zeus Arrhenothelus*, whilst his very early poem, *The Tale of Archais,* published in 1898, features a young man who prays to Aphrodite to be turned into a beautiful girl so that he can lure Zeus' attention away from his lover, the girl called Archais. This bisexuality was not just theoretical. Crowley believed that, during one of his past lives, he had been a temple prostitute called Astarte at Agrigentum in Sicily. Equally, on New Year's Day 1899, the mage travelled astrally into the past and, in a woman's form, had a sexual encounter with the lesbian poet Sappho. It follows, then, that he took pains to develop within himself the magical qualities of the Whore of Babylon, even to the extent of adopting the 'female role' in his sex magic operations- he was a great advocate for the magical power that was generated by anal sex. Crowley had a female alter ego called Alys and wanted his epitaph to be "half a woman made with half a god."[35]

Crowley elaborated on these ideas in the *Book of Thoth*, when describing the Fool card of the tarot. Zeus is known to have cross-dressed from time to time (as did other figures in Greek myth, such as Herakles). Such an androgyne figure seems to have symbolised a primordial perfection, the synthesis of opposites and the union of heaven and earth. Crowley, however, took this idea much further. He wrote:

> "*Zeus Arrhenothelus*: In dealing with Zeus, one is immediately confronted with this deliberate confusion of the masculine and the feminine. In the Greek and Latin traditions, the same thing happens. Dianus and Diana are twins and lovers; as soon as one utters the feminine, it leads

35 Booth, *Magick Life*, 314; Churton, *Aleister Crowley*, 47–48.

> on to the identification with the masculine, and vice versa, as must be the case in view of the biological facts of nature. It is only in Zeus Arrhenothelus that one gets the true hermaphroditic nature of the symbol in unified form. This is a very important fact… because images of this god recur again and again in alchemy. It is hardly possible to describe this lucidly; the idea pertains to a faculty of the mind which is 'above the Abyss;' but all two-headed eagles with symbols clustering about them are indications of this idea. The ultimate sense seems to be that the original god is both male and female, which is, of course, the essential doctrine of the Qabalah; and the thing most difficult to understand about the later, debased, Old Testament tradition is that it represents Tetragrammaton as masculine, in spite of the two feminine components…"

Crowley then moved on to examine several of Zeus' divine sons, touching on some of the areas we have already considered, but also bringing out the hermaphrodite or bisexual nature of the gods:

> *"Dionysus Zagreus/Bacchus Diphues:* It is convenient to treat the two gods as one. Zagreus is only important… [because] he possesses horns, and because (in the Eleusinian Mysteries) it is said that he was torn to pieces by the Titans. But Athena rescued his heart and carried it to his father, Zeus. His mother was Demeter; he is thus the fruit of the marriage of Heaven and Earth…
>
> *Bacchus Diphues*… represents a more superficial form of worship; the ecstasy characteristic of the god is more magical than mystical. The latter demands the name *Iacchus*, whereas Bacchus had Semele for a mother, who was visited by Zeus in the form of a flash of lightning which destroyed her. But she was already pregnant by him, and Zeus saved

> the child. Until puberty, he was hidden in the 'thigh' (i.e. the phallus) of Zeus. Hera, in revenge for her husband's infidelity with Semele, drove the boy mad…
>
> The legend of *Bacchus* is, first of all, that he was *Diphues*, double-natured, and this appears to mean more bisexual than hermaphroditic. His madness is also a phase of his intoxication, for he is pre-eminently the god of the vine. He goes dancing through Asia, surrounded by various companions, all insane with enthusiasm; they carry staffs headed with pine cones and entwined with ivy; they also clash cymbals, and in some legends are furnished with swords, or twined about with serpents. All the half-gods of the forest are the male companions of the Maenad women… In the legend of his journey through Asia, he is said to have ridden on an ass, which connects him with Priapus, who is said to have been his son by Aphrodite… In the worship of Bacchus there was a representative of the god, and he was chosen for his quality as a young and virile, but effeminate man."

In addition, we may note that in *Magick in Theory and Practice,* Crowley also referred to Bacchus-Dionysos as "an effeminate figure," a gentle, exquisite youth with a meek personality – yet with horns concealed beneath his ivy wreath. He labelled him, too, the "twy-formed, man-woman," "doubly-double" in nature. In all these descriptions of the god, Crowley perceived and pulled together several of the themes of this book, for example the sexual aspects of Dionysos and his overlap with numerous other gods. The author also demonstrated the breadth of his knowledge of classical and occult texts. Had he been more focussed in his activities and his writing, Crowley could have had some remarkable achievements. As it was, he sadly dissipated his energies in his addictions to sex and drugs and spent far more of his time building up his image as the 'Wickedest Man in the World.'[36]

36 Crowley, *Magick in Theory & Practice*, 1976, 13 & 263.

Summary

When Crowley died, poor and sick, in a Hastings guest-house in 1947, his life's work might have been deemed a failure. Most of his books were unpublished or out of print, many of his writings had been lost or destroyed, and the general public were – in the main – ignorant of or indifferent to his ideas – unless, of course, they recalled the outrageous falsehoods and exaggerations disseminated against him by the tabloid press. In retrospect, too, it was hard to like Crowley as a person. He could undoubtedly be charming and was extremely witty and erudite company. He was, too, vindictive, conceited and selfish, and he often treated ex-lovers and collaborators terribly. Nevertheless, we must see beyond these personal defects to his work. It may have seemed irrelevant in 1947, but things changed quite quickly – within only a couple of decades.

Since the late 1960s, Crowley's reputation has been substantially rehabilitated and many scholars – as well as occultists – are taking a serious interest in his writings and practices. Crowley appreciated the energy of the Dionysian cult and reintroduced this into modern magick. Whilst it may be recalled that in classical Greek worship of Dionysos, sexuality played a definite role but was not seen as central to contact with the god, Crowley diverged from that aspect of ancient tradition and practice by granting sex a much greater potency and significance. In this respect, his responses to the Dionysian rites seem to be reflective of the general modern understanding of the god and his cult. Crowley's thoughts on Dionysos were deeply, if idiosyncratic; they were embedded within his theories and, as such, they and their application in his rites are deserving of study, as they are likely to be of continuing influence upon our perceptions of the god.

An excellent summary of Crowley's character – and of his relationship to Dionysian practice – came from his friend, the writer and publisher James Cleugh. "It is true that he repeatedly gave himself up to orgy. But never with frenzy or sheer helplessness. He was too good a Greek scholar for that."[37]

DIONYSOS IN THE NEW FOREST

> "Our Dionysian morality is not 'safety first', but 'vitality first."[38]

In the period after the First World War, individuals who disliked the apparent militarism and imperialism of the Boy Scout movement set up several rival outdoor youth organisations: the Order of Woodcraft Chivalry, the Kindred of the Kibbo Kift and the Woodcraft Folk. These new groups returned to some of the founding ideas of scouting – the 'regeneration of the Anglo-Saxon race' through the 'woodcraft' system of open-air life and outdoor education that had been pioneered at the start of the twentieth century by Ernest Thompson Seton. To these ideas the groups added their own distinctive philosophies, drawing on pacifism, psychology, spirituality, art and politics, in order to provide unique camping experiences for all genders and ages. In particular, each group developed detailed and sometimes unorthodox ideas about "sex instruction" and "sex equality" interlinked with their complex theories on camping.

These alternative scouting movements appealed to both the children of communists, socialists and less committed working-class families and also to the growing armies of the unemployed. Atheists found their lack of connections to established churches appealing. To add to these attractions, in their writings and philosophies, these early groups sometimes mixed a strong sensual and sexual message with their other ideas.

---

37 K. Grant, *Remembering Aleister Crowley*, 1991, 33.
38 Harry Byngham.

The Order of Woodcraft Chivalry (OWC) was the first pacifist splinter movement to break away from Scouts; it was established by geologist, anthropologist and Quaker Ernest Westlake in 1916 and was at its most productive and influential in the 1920s and 1930s, with public projects that included the progressive Forest School for children, and the *Grith Fyrd* (Anglo-Saxon for Peace Army) craft training camp for unemployed men during the thirties. A founding motto was "In order to become spiritual, one must first be natural."

In 1919 Westlake, motivated by Seton's Woodcraft Indian movement, bought the Sandy Balls estate as a site for his newly formed OWC. Sandy Balls is on the northern edge of the New Forest in Hampshire, just east of Fordingbridge. The resort has never stopped growing and attracting camping visitors and, even today, its philosophical roots based on woodcraft remain part of its ambience.

The OWC took the English knight rather than the Native American warrior as its mythic ideal, and included adults as well as girls and boys. Based from 1920 at Sandy Balls, the group's colourful, ceremonial camp practices attracted thousands of members in the interwar years. The group was committed to an outdoor life, a belief in the capacity of children to self-govern, and a biologically-inspired developmental model of recapitulation, which proposed that children should perform, or recapitulate, all successive stages of cultural evolution, from the undeveloped 'primitive' to a 'civilised' maturity. The aim was to "regain Paradise – a state of harmony with all creation." The Order believed that profound social, cultural and spiritual change was needed to correct the multiple ills besetting a war-torn nation. Militarism and materialist consumerism were damaging modern society and only a return to the best of the past could create a foundation for the new future they envisaged. Camping was seen as a return to basics which helped make members simple and hardy and so led to moral, physical and spiritual rebirth.

Ernest Westlake

Despite being a Quaker, Ernest Westlake was inspired by the writings of classical scholar Jane Ellen Harrison (1850–1928) on ecstatic Greek religion. In her two books, *Themis – A Study of the Social Origins of Greek Religion* (1912) and *Ancient Art and Ritual* (1913), she examined worship of Dionysos as the *encautos daimon,* the vegetation god. This resonated deeply with Westlake and formed the basis of his vision and philosophy for the OWC. He declared "our movement is a Dionysos movement," striving against "the *cul de sac* of intellectualised religion."

At the OWC's annual Folkmoot in 1921, the desire was expressed to honour Westlake as the founder by bestowing a ceremonial name upon him. He proposed that he should be called the Jack-in-the-Green, from the leaf-clad figure in English May Day processions. He saw himself as the living representative of the vegetation spirit and the Jack in the Green as the exact counterpart of Dionysos, the spirit of the return to nature. In the event, it was decided, rather prosaically, to call him 'The Father of the Order.'[39]

Westlake was killed in a car accident in Holborn in 1922, before he could develop his ideas much further. However, in 1927, the Council of Chiefs of the OWC decided to publish some of their late founder's writings, both because they were intrinsically of interest and because they might guide the development of the movement. They were clear, though, that "neither the Order as a whole nor its Council of Chiefs has come to any definite conclusion on this subject, as to how it should be stated and incorporated in the Order's official policy and aim."

Of particular interest to us here is the pamphlet entitled The *Place of Dionysos* (number nine of the 'Woodcraft Way' series). This gathered together a number of documents and letters that Westlake had written, giving them some degree of coherence.

---

39 *The Place of Dionysos*, 20–21 & 23.

Even so, given the nature of the materials, the arguments are not entirely systematic and there is some repetition. The *Place of Dionysos* is still extremely valuable, though, as it provides a concise statement of a modern understanding and application of the Dionysian rites.[40]

The pamphlet begins with some inspirational quotes, which include *The Bacchae* and some lines from William Blake's *Songs of Innocence.* An editorial note follows, written by the founder's son, Dr Aubrey Westlake. This is headed by a few lines from *Songs of the Groves* by Victor Neuburg, which had been printed in the Woodcraft journal, *Pine Cone.*

> "They called me never:
> But Dionysus came,
> Whence earth forever
> Is lighted by my flame."[41]

Dr Westlake went on to reveal that "ever since the Order's inception in 1916, there has been hidden away, here and there in a little sentence or phrase, a hint of its Dionysian character, but so much in the background has this remained that when… the fact was made explicit, it was received with astonishment and a certain amount of questioning." In light of this, he felt that it was time for a more comprehensive statement of his father's ideas. Aubrey Westlake then made several significant statements. Firstly, "Woodcraft has a two-fold aspect: a primitive backwoodsman or Pan-Artemis aspect and an artistic return-to-nature, or Dionysian." The former was now very well served by boy-scouting and girl-guiding, but the second was largely forgotten or was suppressed because it was not considered respectable. Yet, Dr Westlake felt that expression of our Dionysian side was essential

40 Foreword to Westlake, *Place of Dionysos*, Godshill, 1927, 3.

41 Taken from 'Night Song of Bacchus' from his collection *Songs of the Groves*, 1921 (see later).

to a person's physical and spiritual health, the latter being sorely neglected at the time, he felt. Then he emphasised:

> "This pamphlet deals with what we call the Woodcraft side of that synthetic conception called "Woodcraft Chivalry." Neither backwoodsman-ship nor its artistic Dionysian counterpart are the be-all and end-all, for balancing them is another side, which we call the Chivalric, embracing the Christian and the Apollonian concepts of life. These, however – already accepted to a greater or lesser extent as integral parts of our modern civilisation – do not require the same emphasis as the tabooed and neglected Dionysian."[42]

We see the influence of Nietzsche here, with his call to redress the equilibrium of modern life by restoring the natural and artistic elements of culture. Dr Westlake predicted an imminent change in human society, an evolution to a higher plane of consciousness characterised by Dionysian love and unity (as we know, what we got was the polar opposite). Then, before turning to his father's writings, the son quoted an extensive passage from Euripides *Bacchae,* a beautiful lyric spoken by the chorus.[43] Rather like Aleister Crowley – and numerous others since – the play was treated as something of a canonical text by Westlake. The rest of the text of *The Place of Dionysos* breaks down into three themes: Ernest Westlake's theories on the nature of Dionysos and his cult; what the Dionysian rites aim to change, and the future mission of the OWC.

What, then, did Dionysos mean in the early twentieth century? Dionysos, "the spirit of the Return to Nature," and Eros, the spirit of love, are regarded as central to the message: both are the spirits of life and of life's ecstasy. At the bacchic revels, both are present, for "*ecstasis,* the shifting of the centre of consciousness, is what is aimed at, and the Bacchanalian excesses or 'orgies' – which may

42 *Place of Dionysos*, 5 & 6.

43 Lines 862–911.

take any form – are for the sake of taking the worshipper 'out of himself,'" which is simply the English meaning of *ecstasis*." The problem is, though, that we have given too much attention to Eros and far too little to the Bacchic aspects. We should be more open to our instincts and impulses. Westlake then laid out what might be regarded as his key message: "The spirit of poetry is the spirit of joy; joy depends upon the satisfaction of instinct… The good is that which makes for life; and while love makes for life… natural surroundings make also for life, and make for it in a more invigorating way…"[44]

In classical times, the Bacchic cult offered a ritual return to nature. What was needed, Westlake believed, was a recovery of the balance between beauty and wildness, between city and country. People needed poetry as well as rationalism and science. They needed to rediscover Dionysos, "the god of all growing things, and of the exuberance and joy of life which pours into those who partake of their fruits, and of the grape in particular- the Christmas feast is not Christian, but Dionysian. His worship consists in a return through excess and ecstasy to the bosom of the nature – from whence man came – to the life of instinct and emotion…" Then, in an almost Taoist manner, he argues that "too great fixity and uniformity are as deadly as too little" and that what we need to develop is "difference and fluidity." This is the way in which the cult of Dionysos will help society to escape from the yoke of tradition and to melt the frost of custom, so giving the human soil a chance to grow something fresh. Humans need to embrace diversity and flexibility.[45]

Ernest Westlake was convinced that what needed to be overthrown was the inheritance of centuries of domination by Rome and the church. Together they had repressed Dionysos and left nothing joyous in the world. They had 'chained down' the human spirit to the "dead level of his ordinary every-day

44 *Place of Dionysos*, 9 & 10.
45 *Place of Dionysos*, 11–13.

consciousness" and had forbidden escape. The only comforts that people had left to them were drugs and sex. The 'enemy' is the spirit of dominance and order. Opposed to this is Dionysos, the spirit of life. The task, then, is "how to make this gentle spirit of nature the ruler."

Luckily, there was a way – and it was a better way:

> "Surely it were better to recognise that Dionysos is a god, the personification of indestructible elements in man, the over-flowing and exuberance of life, leading to excess, to breaking out and away from the customary and going back to nature out of one's normal consciousness. Dionysos stands for the pressure of life against its surroundings, the instinctive effort to surpass ourselves. To mingle with the Universe, and feel what we cannot express but cannot conceal – that is a part of religion – the religion of the future, for to progress is to be 'extra' to something. More than for change of air, change of place, change of scene, change of occupation, the mind longs to escape at times from its everyday self and to undergo the radical change which the ancients knew as *ecstasis*, and which was the goal of most of their ritual… the Bacchic rites were the way by which an over-civilised people might regain for a time their kinship with the sub-human and super-human world and their own immemorial past. If the moderns cannot, it will only show that their civilisation has passed the point of recovery. For without such home-going to his mother's breast, there can be no refreshment of man's spirit, no new poetry nor art."[46]

What was the role of the OWC in this? Here, Westlake made some startling and bold statements. "The *Bacchae* is simply a contest between civilisation (materialism) and Woodcraft… the deadening effect of one being contrasted with the vitalising

46 *Place of Dionysos*, 14-18.

influence of the other... our Movement is a Dionysos movement... if we in the Order use this knowledge, we shall obtain great light from a study of the Hellenic developments of the original movement- we shall not only see what we are, but what we should be and how to obtain it." In fact, Westlake saw the OWC as, in effect, the priests of nature, reviving poetry and the bacchanalian spirit. The ultimate aim was this: "As the Dionysos worship revived old Hellas, so may the same thing, introduced by the Order of Woodcraft Chivalry, revive the greater Hellas of modern civilisation."[47]

In 1921 Westlake declared that the 'Trinity of Woodcraft' consisted of Pan, Artemis and Dionysos. Pan represented the semi-animal spirit of the wild. Artemis was the spirit of the woodlands, which he saw as humans' first home. Dionysos/Iacchos was, as we have seen, the spirit of the escape from the cities and the return to nature. Westlake proposed that this new trinity should be adopted by the OWC, with each god appropriate to a different age group of the membership, with Pan for the children and Dionysos for the adults. Through each, members would experience rapture and be able to reconnect with their older, instinctual selves.[48]

Westlake also proposed that Aphrodite should be revered at appropriate times, pointing out that – unless alcohol and sexuality were honoured responsibly and treated as sacred – they could manifest themselves in drunkenness and prostitution. Westlake contemplated, but did not proceed with, a newspaper advertisement stating that an "ex-Quaker wishes to unite with some heathen church in England worshipping the gods, especially Venus and Bacchus."

The Place of Dionysos is short, only twenty-four pages long. However, it is a densely argued manifesto for achieving a better world through the medium of the Dionysian rite. It's a passionate

47 *Place of Dionysos*, 21.
48 *Place of Dionysos*, 22–23.

and inspiring document and one may well wish that Westlake had lived longer to be able to develop and record his thoughts more fully. Even so, in the reading list that's appended to *The Place of Dionysos,* we may get some clue as to what more he might have said. It includes, as we might expect, Nietzsche (*The Birth of Tragedy, The Will to Power* and *Thus Spake Zarathustra*) alongside works by Edward Carpenter, Freud, Jung and Rabindranath Tagore. One recommendation is sexologist Havelock Ellis' *Dance of Life,* which promotes self-development through the arts; another is *The Candle of Vision* by Æ (William Russell), a work on nature mysticism. Perhaps understandably, there's also fiction and poetry, such as works by George Bernard Shaw, Walt Whitman, Algernon Blackwood's *Pan's Garden*, and James Stephen's modern Irish faery tale, *The Crock of Gold.*

> "We stript and, talking in the wood
> As far before in Plato's time,
> We found anew how Good was good
> And how the world is one...
> Anew the bare skin on the grass,
> The free hair twisting in the wind..."[49]

More broadly, the Order explored personal development, focussing upon nudism, sex reform, and sex education for children. A range of radical ideas were proposed, including much more relaxed attitudes towards cohabitation, open marriages, bisexuality and homosexuality. Naturism and frankness about sexual matters were thought to be the best means of dealing with repression and shame. At the Priory Gate woodcraft school in Norfolk naked exercise and the use of naked child members as models for life drawing classes caused alarm to more conservative members of the Order. The liberated and liberal approach of

49 One of two poems by Victor Neuburg published in the *Pine Cone*, October 1923.

some in the OWC is demonstrated firstly by leading member Dorothy Revel, who would strip naked except for her shoes to demonstrate dance works such as Jacques Offenbach's *Orpheus in the Underworld* to young members. It need hardly be said that very few of Westlake's radical ideas and practices sat well with the Quaker roots of the Order.

Harry Byngham

After Westlake died, the role of Chief of the Order fell to Harry Byngham, who subsequently changed his name to Dion, short for Dionysos. Byngham was a natural health journalist and disciple of William Blake, Walt Whitman and Nietzsche. Unlike Westlake, Dion Byngham found no attraction at all in Christianity; for example, at the 1923 summer's camp at Sandy Balls, he challenged the singing of Christian hymns and asked instead for readings from Edward Carpenter or William Blake (perhaps indicating his influence on the bibliography and quotations included in *The Place of Dionysos*). He set about zealously promoting paganism, naturism and phallic worship as a veneration of the life force. For him, the ecstatic Bacchic revels offered a template for living a joyous life close to the earth. The Order adopted the thyrsos as its visual symbol, the phallic ivy-wreathed wand topped with a pine cone. Dionysos represented the animal part of manhood for Byngham, a quality he began to promote.

Byngham started publishing an Order periodical called *The Pine Cone*, which contained many provocative items, including a nude Dionysus wielding a thyrsos on the cover of one issue and two poems as well as a verse play celebrating the goddess Diana that were written by Victor Neuburg, a former close associate of Aleister Crowley who introduced Byngham to the ideas of the famous occultist. In his (brief) role as editor of the journal, Byngham explained to readers that the pine cone of the title represented not only the cones strewn about Sandy Balls camp site but was also the head of a penis. He declared that the Order "should be proud to regard itself as the erect penis of the... nation or civilisation of which it is a part."

In the first issue of the *Pine Cone,* Byngham called for:

> "the realisation of Life ... Life is adventure, audacity, revolt ... life springs out of the star-tissued womb of Nature as the virile son of the All-Mother. Life seeks reunion or religion with Nature, his mother, not, however, by falling back into her arms and surrendering once more to some primordial slumber and dream, but by striving away from and with her, searching her, playing with her, dancing before her, wooing her, overcoming her, until she, who is eternally young as well as eternally old, responds like a maiden to his life and will and power, and, in the transfiguring ecstasy of union a new cosmic consciousness is conceived."

Byngham declared that he wanted to give the movement a 'Physical Basis,' by which he meant "the idea and practice of getting as closely as possible into direct bodily contact with Nature's elements – earth, water, wind and sunlight – and the progressive acquisition of the mental attitude which makes this affirmation of bodily liberation, health, beauty and freedom possible. Freedom – individually and socially – is vastly and infinitely more important than stuffy regard for convention or 'village prudery.'" He realised he would have to "shock and hurt some people" but he pressed ahead with his vision of a new moral order, promoting nude bathing, eugenics, sexual experimentation and nudism as a cure for psychiatric problems.

Byngham's application of Dionysian ideas profoundly challenged the Order's wish to be respectable. For example, his advocacy of gymnosophy, or social nudism, resulted in risqué articles in *Pine Cone,* illustrated with naked photographs of him and his girlfriend as pan pipe-playing nymphs. Byngham's cohabitation before marriage was also a source of consternation. His last offence involved dancing naked with his lover in front of journalists, in a performance that aimed to be the embodiment of ecstasy. For this flagrant challenge to sexual propriety, Byngham was dismissed as editor in 1924, after only four issues, and was suspended by the Order in 1925.

Active around the very same time in the New Forest area was Gerald Gardner, founder of British Wicca. He was certainly influenced by Byngham's thinking, and there is some evidence that they may have met. Some of Byngham's innovations at the OWC, such as a quartered ritual circle, a three-stage initiation, a horned god, a moon goddess and ritual nudity, can be identified in Gardner's thought too. Certainly, after his brief spell with the OWC, Byngham moved to Storrington in Sussex where he lived on a commune called The Sanctuary, promoting free-love, paganism, nudism, sun-worship, magic and Dionysian rites. Aleister Crowley's former partner, Victor Neuburg, lived nearby in Steyning.

Byngham continued to worship a trinity of Pan, Artemis and Dionysus (an idea initially formulated by Quaker Westlake), with Dionysos representing life and the animal side of human nature. He contributed to the magazine, *Healthy Life,* appearing in one edition performing a naked Nature Prayer Dance for Pan. In the 1930s Byngham wrote a series of 'Pan Pamphlets', such as 'Creative Simplicity,' as well as collections of verse, such as *Sonnets and Songs* and *Living Moments* (1980). The 'Pan Pamphlets' were published by the Bureau of Cosmotherapy, based improbably in the Surrey market town of Leatherhead. This seems to have been run by Florrie and John Mahon as part of their International Health and Education Centre and the League of Health and Healing. Other Pan Pamphlets included guides to the thought of Zoroaster and Buddha by Edmond Szekely (Director of the International Cosmotherapeutic Expedition); the Bureau also issued *Cosmovitalist Monthly*.

VERSE

As we have seen from the competitions held at his ancient festivals, as well as from the theories of Nietzsche, poetry has always been very closely associated with Dionysos/Bacchus. The god is the source of inspiration, most especially through wine, and both wine and women are subjects seen as being particularly fitted to praise in verse. So intimate is this link that one Greek author, Anacreon, and the style of poetry he is supposed to have invented – called 'Anacreontic' – are inseparable from the god and his sponsored pleasures. Little verse that was authentically written by Anacreon survives, but we do have one *Hymn to Dionysos*:

> "Roving god, whose playfellows
> Over the mountains' airy brows
> In happy chase are led;
> Where Love, who breaks the heart of pride,
> Or nymphs amuse you, violet-eyed,
> Or Aphrodite keeps your side –
> The goddess rosy-red –
> Lord Dionysos, I kneel to thee;
> Stoop to me in your charity
> And this my prayer receive:
> Dear Lord, your best persuasion use,
> Bid Cleobulus not refuse
> The gift of love I give."

The young god's indissoluble links to the 'triple worship' of wine, women and the muses are underlined in other, later bacchanalian and love verses that are now ascribed to Anacreon; for example:

> "For all your life, old man, was poured out as an offering to these three – the Muses, Dionysos and Eros [in other words, he indulged solely in music, wine and love]."

> "I owe many thanks, Dionysos [wine], for having escaped Eros' bonds completely, bonds made harsh by Aphrodite."
>
> "Lord Dionysos, with whom Eros the subduer, the blue-eyed nymphs, and radiant Aphrodite play, as you haunt the lofty mountain peaks."[50]

The God Revived

Elizabeth Barrett Browning (1806–61) was often drawn to the power and symbolism of classical myth, but she always wrote from the standpoint of a triumphant and evangelical church. Her *Dead Pan* of 1844 contemplated how the birth and later resurrection of Jesus had inevitably resulted in the downfall, into irrelevance, of the former Olympian gods. Her poem addresses each deity almost mockingly and Dionysos – who was for her a false saviour – is not spared:

> "Bacchus, Bacchus! on the panther
> He swoons- bound with his own vines!
> And his maenads slowly saunter,
> Head aside, among the pines,
> While they murmur dreamingly-
> "Evohe – ah – evohe!
> Ah, Pan is dead."

Yet, even as Browning wrote, a sea change was occurring. As early as the start of the century, Shelley and Leigh Hunt had set up an altar to Pan in the woods at Marlow during Shelley's residency there. By the beginning of the succeeding century, the church's position looked far less secure, its victory far less final.

In *Reveille* (1908) the poet Michael Field (who was really Katherine Harris Bradley and her niece and ward Edith Emma Cooper) imagined a spring sacrifice to the god. He is

50 Anacreon, *Fragments* 12, 346 & 357.

summoned back to life on the shores of the Alcyonian Lake in the Peloponnese, a site traditionally regarded as a point of entry into the underworld and the location from which Dionysos departed in search of his mother, Semele. A black lamb, decorated with flowers, is sacrificed (by drowning rather than by shedding blood). The god is seen to brighten and flash on the water, which is then scooped up to water vineyards and meadows. What Field seems to have wished to achieve here was, firstly, to tone down the Dionysian ceremonies for a modern readership by removing bloody sacrifice and the eating of raw flesh and, secondly, to suppress the personal deity, making Dionysos merely immanent in the natural world. This loses an essential part of the cult but makes the scene more Christian in tone.

In 1912 R.C. Trevelyan dramatised the story of Ariadne in blank verse in *The Bride of Dionysus.* The cast includes maenads, satyrs and nereids on the island of Naxos' "satyr-haunted shores/ Where roams the fierce night-revelling Maenad rout." In the text, Trevelyan sought to express the power and attraction of the ancient cult. Dionysus describes how his frenzy affects his followers:

> "In these alone, as in a chosen temple,
> His godhead entering and possessing dwells.
> An inward kindling presence felt, an ecstasy
> A quickening and transforming power..."

Later, the deity expresses the deeper meaning of his mystery- that it is concerned with rebirth and resurrection: "... my vintage/ Not from the bitter earth-born grapes of Death/But pressed forth from the Vine of Life, even then/Drunken, though thou knewest not, was thy soul." Ariadne understands this and declares "O Dionysus, thee the world's life, the world's glory/With the fullness of thy Godhead made whole!"

D.H. Lawrence mused upon the role of Dionysos as a god of rebirth in his poem, 'Medlars and Sorb Apples,' from the collection *Birds, Beasts and Flowers* published in 1923. Eating the 'bletted' fruit provoked for him a deep meditation on divinity and death:

"What is it, in the grape turning raisin,
In the medlar, in the sorb-apple,
Wineskins of brown morbidity,
Autumnal excrementa;
What is it that reminds us of white gods?

Gods nude as blanched nut-kernels...
And drenched with mystery.

Sorb-apples, medlars with dead crowns,
I say, wonderful are the hellish experiences,
Orphic, delicate,
Dionysos of the Underworld...

Going down the strange lanes of hell, more and more
intensely alone,
The fibres of the heart parting one after the other
And yet the soul continuing, naked-footed, ever more
vividly embodied
Like a flame blown whiter and whiter
In a deeper and deeper darkness,
Ever more exquisite, distilled in separation.

So, in the strange retorts of medlars and sorb-apples
The distilled essence of hell."

Eating the fruit with a glass of wine evoked a sense of "Orphic farewell,"

> "And the ego sum of Dionysos
> The *sono io* of perfect drunkenness
> Intoxication of final loneliness."

The revival of awareness of the deeper meanings of Bacchus/Dionysos was an important development in European culture, but it occurred at a time when both native folk traditions and classical myth were, simultaneously, being popularised and thereby diminished and trivialised. The same societies that could be fascinated by what the ancient gods had to offer – and which drew dramatic and artistic inspiration from them – could at the same time prettify and emasculate those very same legends and symbols. *Bacchus* by Canadian poet Francis Joseph Sherman (1871–1926) may be seen as an example of this: the god is discovered to have come back again with his 'precious draught,' but he is heard "Growling at his fairy host" and turns to be just a honey-bee "Revelling within a rose!" This criticism notwithstanding, the verse still serves to underline the close association of the god with Nature, an ancient aspect of his character that should not be forgotten. Madison Julius Cawein, a poet of the natural world who was often called the 'Keats of Kentucky,' also enhanced this link when he described Indian turnips "As if some woodland Bacchus there/While braiding locks of hyacinth hair/With ivy-tod, had idly tost/His thyrsus down."[51]

Then again, perhaps Sherman knew more than he revealed in his verse. Art and literary critic Walter Pater in 1895 wrote this of the bacchic dances:

> "It is to such ecstasies, however, that all nature-worship seems to tend; that giddy, intoxicating sense of spring- that tingling in the veins, sympathetic with the yearning life of the earth, having, apparently, in all times and places, prompted some mode of wild dancing. Coleridge, in one

51 Cawein, *Forest & Field.*

> of his fantastic speculations, refining on the German word for enthusiasm – *Schwärmerei*, swarming, as he says, "like the swarming of bees together" – has explained how the sympathies of mere numbers, as such, the random catching on fire of one here and another there, when people are collected together, generates as if by mere contact, some new and rapturous spirit, not traceable in the individual units of a multitude. Such swarming was the essence of that strange dance of the Bacchic women: literally like winged things, they follow, with motives, we may suppose, never quite made clear even to themselves, their new, strange, romantic god."[52]

The Canadian writer Lucy Maud Montgomery (1874–1942) made similar connections to Sherman between Greek mythology and faery tradition in her poem 'The Forest Path.' A walk in the woods elicits for her thoughts of "old romance:"

> "Down into the forest dipping,
> Deep and deeper as we go,
> One might fancy dryads slipping
> Where the white-stemmed birches grow.
>
> Lurking gnome and freakish fairy
> In the fern may peep and hide;
> Sure their whispers low and airy
> Ring us in on every side!
>
> Saw you where the pines are rocking
> Nymph's white shoulder as she ran?
> Lo, that music faint and mocking,
> Is it not a pipe of Pan?

52 W. Pater, *Greek Studies*, 56-57.

Hear you that elusive laughter
Of the hidden waterfall?
Nay, a satyr speeding after
Ivy-crowned bacchanal.

Far and farther as we wander
Sweeter shall our roaming be,
Come, for dim and winsome yonder
Lies the path to Arcady!"

What this poem also demonstrates rather well is the manner in which Pan and his satyrs and nymphs easily become jumbled together, fairly indiscriminately, with the Dionysian rites and the young god's mortal followers as well as with the faes.

Even though a pagan revival had taken place, it has still had to contend with the longstanding equation between Bacchus/ Dionysos and Christ. Australian poet Bernard O'Dowd hymned the god Bacchus because he elevates his adherents through the vine, and also through the verse that drunkenness can evoke:

"I am the gift of tongues that flame
Inspired resolve above:
I wither the weeds of paltry aim
That choke the growth of love."

He's aware of the hazards of indulgence, but controls himself by focussing upon the higher goal that he has in mind:

"Though sometimes through forbidden gates,
The drugged and drunken may
Intrude among initiates
And misconceive the play,

No self-indulgence walks my stage;
My frenzies make divine...
A eucharist my wine:"

O'Dowd avoids the "stews of maudlin gluttony" and partakes of the creative impulse that has fired all writers throughout history- from Savonarola to Nietzsche. It is at this point, with his reference to the Italian preacher, that his subtext is revealed. Rather like Elizabeth Barrett Browning, he proceeds by declaring that "The old gods shuddered; for they saw/Their altar flames expire/Before the breath of a Higher Law/That crucifies Desire." O'Dowd's *Bacchus* was really a metaphor for the son of god, the old deity having been vanquished by the 'light.' This is not a hymn, therefore, but an epitaph, and quite a triumphalist one.

Nevertheless, many could see the contemporary relevance of the ancient divinity and could conceive of themselves communing with him, not in far-off imagined Greece but in the familiar landscapes of their home counties. Thus, James Elroy Flecker quite easily conjured maenads on the Cotswolds:

"When I go down the Gloucester lanes
My friends are deaf and blind:
Fast as they turn their foolish eyes
The Maenads leap behind,
And when I hear the fire-winged feet,
They only hear the wind.
Have I not chased the fluting Pan
Through Cranham's sober trees?
Have I not sat on Painswick Hill
With a nymph upon my knees,
And she as rosy as the dawn,
And naked as the breeze?"[53]

53 Flecker, from *Oak & Olive*.

In pastoral and unspoilt countryside, others too could conjure up Arcadian images of the god and his retinue, as Francis Palgrave did in his *Dorset Idyl*:

> "Green Dorset winds his holy vale,
> Where the divine deep nightingale
> Heaps note on note and love on love,
> In ivy thick unseen,
> While goddesses with Dionysos rove."

Matthew Arnold similarly found maenads present in the celebrations of young men and women in the hayfields after harvest.[54]

One poet above all, perhaps, was committed to seeking to revive the meaning and vitality of the classical gods in the modern world- and that was Oscar Wilde. The author regarded Dionysos as one of the "most deeply suggestive figures of Greek Mythology" because his birth was directly linked to the death of his mortal mother Semele. His life was the origin of tragedy, in other words- and for this reason Wilde kept a small statue of the god on his desk. For Wilde, "young Dionysos" was an active but potentially dangerous god. He liked to hunt with the bassarids but shared the faults that beset all the Olympians, meaning that he could be vindictive if he felt that his privacy had been violated by mortals.[55]

In 1881 Wilde wrote two poems in which he contemplated the Olympians' return. *Santa Decca* accepted that the ancient gods were dead, but expressed a hope that this might be mistaken. However, Wilde's long poem of that year, *The Burden of Itys,* resolutely transferred all the characters and wonder of Arcady to new lives on the banks of the Thames at Oxford and in the surrounding hills of Cumnor and Bagley Wood. The poet had

54 Matthew Arnold, *Bacchanalia*.
55 Wilde, *De Profundis*, 61; *Charmides*.

realised that he felt closer to true divinity there than he had ever felt in a church during a service.

> "But sweeter far if silver-sandalled foot
> Of some long-hidden God should ever tread
> The Nuneham meadows, if with reeded flute
> Pressed to his lips some Faun might raise his head
> By the green water-flags, ah! sweet indeed..."

The Olympian deities were all within tantalising reach of the poet. By the river-

> "diadems
> Of brown bee-studded orchids which were meant
> For Cytheraea's brows are hidden here
> Unknown to Cytheraea [Aphrodite], and by yonder
> pasturing steer...
>
> [whilst gossamer] seems to bring diviner memories
> Of faun-loved Heliconian glades and blue nymph-haunted seas..."

Though in the English summer countryside, Wilde was surrounded by:

> "memories/ Of Oreads peeping through the leaves of silent moonlit trees,
> Of lonely Ariadne on the wharf
> At Naxos, when she saw the treacherous crew
> Far out at sea, and waved her crimson scarf
> And called false Theseus back again nor knew
> That Dionysos on an amber pard
> Was close behind her..."

In short, the poet confidently declared that:

"well I know they are not dead at all,
The ancient Gods of Grecian poesy:
They are asleep, and when they hear thee call
Will wake and think 't is very Thessaly..."

England then would be alive with the characters of myth:

"Sing on! sing on! let the dull world grow young,
Let elemental things take form again,
And the old shapes of Beauty walk among
The simple garths and open crofts...

Sing on! sing on! and Bacchus will be here
Astride upon his gorgeous Indian throne,
And over whimpering tigers shake the spear
With yellow ivy crowned and gummy cone,
While at his side the wanton Bassarid
Will throw the lion by the mane and catch the mountain kid!

Sing on! and I will wear the leopard skin,
And steal the mooned wings of Ashtaroth,
Upon whose icy chariot we could win
Cithaeron in an hour ere the froth[56]
Has over-brimmed the wine-vat or the Faun
Ceased from the treading! ay, before the flickering lamp of dawn

Has scared the hooting owlet to its nest,
And warned the bat to close its filmy vans,
Some Maenad girl with vine-leaves on her breast
Will filch their beech-nuts from the sleeping Pans
So softly that the little nested thrush
Will never wake, and then with shrilly laugh and leap will rush

56 Ashtaroth is a Phoenician form of Aphrodite; Kithairon is a Greek mountain god also known as Nysos, who was foster-father of Dionysos.

Down the green valley where the fallen dew
Lies thick beneath the elm and count her store,
Till the brown Satyrs in a jolly crew
Trample the loosestrife down along the shore,
And where their horned master sits in state
Bring strawberries and bloomy plums upon a wicker crate!"

Wilde imagined himself surrounded by Pan, Aphrodite and all the nymphs until – in a shattering moment – the dream was dispersed and he found himself back in the Oxford of the late Victorian Britain, "And from the copse left desolate and bare/ Fled is young Bacchus with his revelry." Instead, there is the homely countryside where students roam and the tolling bells that call him back to the High Street and to Christ Church gate. Nonetheless, his return to the familiar world leaves him feeling bereft: "Drifting with every wind on the wide sea of misery."

The God of the Grape

"Bacchus is a dream's dream."[57]

We must begin with a poem by Victor Neuburg, companion of Aleister Crowley and contributor to the OWC bulletin, the *Pine Cone.* Neuburg published at least seven books of poetry and contributed his work as well to Crowley's *Equinox* as well as to literary journals. Egyptian and classical gods are a constant theme in his verse, with poems addressed to Isis, Osiris, Diana, Venus and Pan.[58] Clearly of interest to us is the *Night Song to Bacchus,* included in his 1921 collection *Songs of the Groves.* It imagines Bacchus, along with Pan and Silenus, passing through a wood at night. The god sings of "his mission and of the impending ecstasy of the Earth." The song runs over several pages, so only a few stanzas will be quoted here:

57 D.H Lawrence, *Grapes.*

58 See https://www.100thmonkeypress.com/biblio/vneuburg/downloads/downloads_vn.htm.

"Ring me a wreath,
O Bacchantes mine,
While the tigers' teeth
Are closing on the vine…

All stars are mine!
Bacchantes hear!
Mine is your wine,
With the kiss behind the ear.

The red flame of vision,
From the lees of wine,
Is mine! Is Elysian!
Is mine! is mine!

Ho! For the bacchanalia
Whereat to boast and bouse…

I was the new god
Of wine and ecstasy
Now I am the true God
Of the Great Sea.

So down through the woods,
Dionysus came;
All the multitudes,
Bowed at his name."

Neuburg fitted in references to *thyrsoi, tympana*, cymbals and to Roman god Liber. His Bacchus promises his followers pleasure-plentiful drink, song, love and sex. All they must do is to be open and accept him. Whilst Neuburg was certainly not the greatest poet, here he captured the spirit of the god precisely.

D.H. Lawrence celebrated Dionysos through his archetypal symbol of the ripened fruit – as did many other more modern poets, taking up an ancient and honoured tradition. The grape can liberate, setting the mind and its creative powers free. Edward George Bulwer-Lytton, in his *Bacchic Hymns to the Image of Death,* declared that we owe a great debt to Bacchus because "The grape is the key that we owe to him/From the gaol of the world to free us." Christoph Friedrich von Schiller (1759–1805) had sung similar praises in *The Gods of Greece:*

"The lively Thyrsos-swinger,
And the wild car the exulting panthers bore,
Announced the presence of the rapture-bringer-
Bounded the Satyr and blithe Faun before;
And Maenads, as the frenzy stung the soul,
Hymned in their maddening dance, the glorious wine-
As ever beckoned to the lusty bowl
The ruddy host divine!"

Bacchus' greatest gift to mankind is his 'spiritual medicine.'

Hilaire Belloc's *Heroic Poem in Praise of Wine* unashamedly and unhesitatingly celebrates the drink's function as "true begetter of all arts that be… privilege of the completely free." The poet calls on us all to "exalt, enthrone, establish and defend/To welcome home mankind's mysterious friend":

"Sing how the Charioteer from Asia came,
And on his front the little dancing flame
Which marked the god-head; Sing the Panther-team,
The gilded thyrsus twirling, and the gleam
Of cymbals through the darkness. Sing the drums.
He comes; the young renewer… comes!

And everywhere as they pass, the Vines! The Vines!
The Vines, the conquering Vines!"

Belloc condemns those who drink water ("the mere beverage of the beast") or gin, sings the praises of the many varieties of grape, and declares that, above all things – "Dead lucre: burnt ambition: Wine is best." He seems to have no time for the Christian analogies with Dionysos; rather, it is winegrowers who are "bottling God the Father in a flask/And leading all Creation down distilled/To one small ardent sphere immensely filled."

Those who despise the vine are rightly to be excluded from all pleasures in Belloc's world view- they cannot share our delight in the prospect that:

"We, when repose demands us, welcomed are
In young white arms, like our great Exemplar
Who, wearied with creation, takes his rest
And sinks to sleep on Ariadne's breast."

The poet's advice to his readers for dealing with teetotallers is extremely simple:

"Forget them! Form the Dionysian ring,
And pulse the ground, and Io, Io, sing…
And, sacramental, raise me the Divine:
Strong brother in God and last companion, Wine."

In *Bacchus* Ralph Waldo Emerson also celebrated the holy power of the grape and of wine that "turns the woe of Night/By its own craft, to a more rich delight." This "joyful juice" is the source of all artistic inspiration and connects the poet with the world, so:

"That I intoxicated,
And by the draught assimilated,
May float at pleasure through all natures;
The bird-language rightly spell,
And that which roses say so well:"

Interestingly, Emerson's wine does not blank out griefs and woes, but rather enables him to recover his youthful past:

> "Pour, Bacchus! the remembering wine;
> Retrieve the loss of me and mine!...
> Haste to cure the old despair;
> Reason in Nature's lotus drenched –
> The memory of ages quenched –
> Give them again to shine;"

This is, perhaps, the melancholy nostalgia of inebriation, when lost loves enjoy a bitter sweet recall. It may, in fact, represent just what Nietzsche discussed: the fact that connecting and reconciling ourselves with past griefs and suffering, we can heal and become more whole.

The writers cited so far all appreciated the more spiritual and creative benefits of drink. The Stuart poet Robert Herrick captured one of the simpler but most abiding aspects of Dionysos-his indissoluble associations with inebriation. The *Hymn to Bacchus* is as true and as recognisable today as it was in 1648:

> "I sing thy praise, Iacchus,
> Who with thy thyrse dost thwack us:
> And yet thou so dost back us
> With boldness, that we fear
> No Brutus ent'ring here,
> Nor Cato the severe.
> What though the lictors threat us,
> We know they dare not beat us,
> So long as thou dost heat us.
> When we thy orgies sing,
> Each cobbler is a king,
> Nor dreads he any thing:
> And though he do not rave,

Yet he'll the courage have
To call my Lord Mayor knave;
Besides, too, in a brave,
Although he has no riches,
But walks with dangling breeches
And skirts that want their stitches,
And shows his naked flitches,
Yet he'll be thought or seen
So good as George-a-Green;
And calls his Blouze, his Queen;
And speaks in language keen.
O Bacchus! let us be
From cares and troubles free;
And thou shalt hear how we
Will chant new Hymnes to thee."

Doubtless many readers will have been thwacked with the god's *thyrsos* at the same time as being made bold and eloquent...

Wine can create amorous as well as literary thoughts – far more often the former, in fact. Clark Ashton Smith's 1942 poem *The Hill of Dionysus* captures the human moment at which wine and sex intersect in the intensity of the present. Two men and a naked woman are together on a hill – a sort of *dejeuner sur l'herbe:*

"The bread is eaten and the wine is poured;
While she, the twice-adored,
Between us lies on the pale autumn grass."

The alcohol brings forth the latent passions lurking beneath and helps to bring about physical and spiritual union that overcomes reservations and anxieties:

"It is the hour of mystical accord,
Of respite, and release

From all that hampers us, from all that frets,
And from the vanity of all regrets,
Where grape and laurel twine,
Once more we drink the Dionysian wine,
Ringed with the last horizon that is Greece."

The Irish-Australian poet Victor James Daley (1858–1905), in his verse *Bacchanalian,* celebrated the same freeing qualities of drink, using explicitly classical imagery:

"I pity him who has not swung
The Thyrsos in the air,
And followed Bacchus, blithe and young,
With vine-leaves in his hair;
And heard the Maenads sing,
And the mad cymbals ring.

I pity those who have to walk
In sober ways and sad,
And keep a guard upon their talk
Lest men should think them mad.
Or careless speech should show
The felon thought below.

When in my goblet, blithe and gay,
The beaded bubbles wink,
For all poor souls like this I pray
That they may learn to drink,
And, like a rose in rain,
Open shut heart and brain.

Who does not drink he does not know,
And he will never find,
What merry fellows live below

The surface of his mind:
These other men to me
Are right good company…

Then let us unto Bacchus sing
Evoe! up and down –
For Bacchus is the wisest king
Whoever wore a crown:
His vine leaves hide from view
More wit than Plato knew."

Daley's vision transcends mere tipsiness to disclose the fundamental liberating nature of Dionysos.

All these positive views notwithstanding, though, others took a more nuanced and perhaps honest approach. Thomas Parnell (1679–1718), in *Bacchus, or the Vines of Lesbos*, celebrated how Bacchus, king of pleasure, who "Charmed the wide world with drink and dances," came with his fauns and revived the ailing vineyards of the Greek island. Then, of course, they enjoyed the fruit of their labours: "They sit to riot on the ground/A vessel stands amidst the ring/And here they laugh, and there they sing." The ultimate result is "nonsense, lust and noise." Some of the satyrs boast outrageously and tell tall tales; some fall to fighting; some think of (non-consensual) sex:

"Here one who saw the nymphs that stood
To peep upon them from the wood,
Steals off, to try if any maid
Be lagging late beneath the shade."

Parnell suggested that each drinker took on the character of one of the animals whose dung was used to restore the vines-becoming swinish, sheep-like and so on. It is not a complimentary conclusion to the poem.

Another eighteenth century English poet, William Shenstone, wrote a short verse titled *Written in a Collection of Bacchanalian Songs* in which he rejected the false courage and risk of confusion engendered by wine in preference for a sober pursuit of the purer intoxication of love. Perhaps Shenstone had a valid point. Drink can lead, of course, to overindulgence and then to regret, as the Greek poet Constantine P Cafavy appreciated:

> "the god leading, in divine glory, with power in his stride;
> Intemperance next; and beside Intemperance,
> Intoxication pours out the satyrs' wine
> from an amphora wreathed in ivy;
> near them, Sweet-wine, the delicate,
> eyes half-closed, soporific,
> and behind come the singers
> Tunemaker and Melody and Reveller –
> the last holding the honoured processional torch
> which he never lets die- and then Ceremony, so modest…"[59]

For all his boisterous celebration of the joys of drink though, Robert Herrick nevertheless fully appreicated that wine can release pent-up desire, but in an unbridled and unfocussed manner:

> "Whither dost thou hurry me,
> Bacchus, being full of thee?
> This way, that way, that way, this –
> Here and there a fresh Love is;
> That doth like me, this doth please;
> Thus a thousand mistresses
> I have now: yet I alone,
> Having all, enjoy not one!"[60]

59 C.P. Cafavy (1863–1933), *The Retinue of Dionysos.*

60 Herrick, *Canticle to Bacchus.*

Partaking of Dionysos' gift can be a bittersweet experience, therefore. Wine and love combined can provoke unhappy emotions as readily as joy, as Vyacheslav Ivanovich Ivanov (1866–1949) demonstrated in his *Vineyard of Dionysos*:

> "Dionysus walks his vineyard, his beloved;
> Two women in dark clothing – two vintagers – follow him.
> Dionysus tells the two mournful guards, the vintagers:
> "Take your sharp knives, my vintners, Grief and Torment;
> Harvest, Grief and Torment, my beloved grapes!
> Gather the blood of scarlet bunches, the tears of my golden clusters –
> Take the victim of bliss to the whetstone of grief,
> The purple of suffering to the whetstone of bliss;
> Pour the fervent liquid of scarlet delights into my ardent grail!"

The English poet Lady Margaret Sackville also took the view that the blessings offered by Bacchus were mixed. Her *Hymn to Dionysus,* written in 1905, discloses a very ambivalent attitude to the god that his devotees feel bound helplessly to pursue. He is "pitiless," "dangerous and difficult," a "god of fire and dew, fiery and cold." Worshippers exult "whilst madness swells each vein" but this frenzy is painful, leading afterwards to grief. They implore the god of wine to bring them forgetfulness.

Sackville's 1911 verse drama *The Wooing of Dionysus* built upon these conflicting emotions. The god arrives on an island where he meets a group of young women. He falls for one, a cow herd called Aglae, but she rejects his advances. Angry at this, he reveals his divine nature, warning her that he is both "lord of mirth" and "lord of madness and of fear and mystery." In refusing him, she has lost a chance of life in heaven and has chosen obscure mortality. Another of the maidens, Erinna, appears at this point and declares her love for him. Dionysos, in his turn, rejects her and resolves to leave the island. Undeterred, Erinna pledges to the god that she will "Pursue thee, and pursue by day and night! Rage with thy Bacchantes – be at least/Present, if all-forgotten, at thy feast." She will "drink the scattered madness thou dost fling/In mystic showers amongst thy following/So shall I find some peace at last." So, for Sackville, the maenad's frenzy was a cruel condition akin to unrequited love – an interpretation of the bacchae's situation that stands in stark contrast to almost every other contemporary view of it – as we shall see shortly. We might, though, recall the way in which the god can mete out madness as punishment (for example to Agave) and view Erinna's plight as being related to this.

We'll conclude this section on a more forlorn note. The grapes of Bacchus don't always guarantee unbridled passion. In 1910, whilst he was still an undergraduate, the future war poet Rupert Brooke attended a 'Bacchus Fest' in Munich. In accordance with its name, participants dressed up in skimpy Greek-style robes, drank wine and, predictably, a large number of them then enjoyed sexual experiences – doubtless very much what the organisers of an event with such a title had hoped to facilitate. Sadly, although he met a young woman, Brooke couldn't quite abandon himself to Dionysian excess. According to his account, he and his carnival bride sat sharing a glass of beer and chatting awkwardly until they went home to their separate beds…[61]

The God of Desire

> "Then what wild Dionysia I, young Bacchanal,/Danced in thy lap!"[62]

Lust, when fired successfully by drink, can even so prove to be a befuddled and undiscriminating thing. Fortunately, perhaps,

61 Brooke, *Letters*, 282.

62 Francis Thompson, *An Anthem of Earth*.

another view of Dionysos focusses upon his sexuality wholly separate from his viticultural links. The occult artist Austin Osman Spare, who for a time collaborated with Aleister Crowley on the magazine *Equinox,* observed that "The necessity of a better life is intoxication, but more and greater things than strong drink intoxicate." What he had in mind is revealed by a confession that on one occasion he had had sex with eighteen women during the course of one night. He called these outbursts "Dionysiac spasms of pan-sexualism", during which he had a vision of "all things fornicating all the time."[63]

In *Siren Bowers and The Triumph of Bacchus*, the English poet Roden Berkeley Wriothesley Noel (1834–94) wrote in highly sensual terms of the god and his entourage. The bowers he described are "halls of pleasure/Flushed with flowers" and those blossoms are explicitly erotic: "some are flushed like delicate fair flesh/Of smooth, soft texture; delicate love-organs/ Impetalled hide, depend their fairy forms." There he imagined himself reclined, whilst a priest "Made offering of fruit to Queen Astarte." This goddess is, of course, another form of Aphrodite, and in accordance with her presence, Noel imagined himself surrounded by "forms of youthful loveliness" luxuriating in a "wanton joy/Of Eros, Io, Hebe, Ganymede/And all the poets tell of Aphrodite." Noel then recalled how the goddess seduced the mortal youth Adonis, who appeared in the guise and dress of the Greek god:

> "young Dionysus
> He seemed, the leader of the company,
> Who lolled in a Chryselephantine car
> Upon a pillow's damson velvet pile;
> An undulating form voluptuous,
> All one warm waved and breathing ivory,
> Aglow with male and female lovelihood,

63 Spare, *The Focus of Life*, 1921.

The yellow panther fur worn negligent
Fondling one shoulder."

Like the god's, the boy's face was "fair and beardless like a maid's" and:

"The soft waved hair vine-filleted; he held
Aloft with one white arm's rare symmetry
A crystal brimmed with blood of grape that hath
Heart like a lucid carbuncle; some fallen
Over his form envermeiled more the rose
Of ample bosom, and love-moulded flank;
The fir-coned thyrsos lying along the shoulder,
And listless fingered by a delicate hand,
The languid eyes dim-dewy with desire.
Some foam-fair, and some amber of deep tone
The company to rear of him, yet nigh,
Fawn-youths and maidens robed in woven wind
Of that fine alien fabric, hiding only
As lucid wave hides, or a vernal haze;
But some were rough and red, and rudely hewn,
Goat-shagged, satyric; all high-held the vine,
(Or quaffed it reeling), and the fir-cone rod;
The fairer filleted with violet,
Anemone, or rose, Adonis-flower,
The rude with vine, or ivy; syrinx, flute,
Sweetly they breathed into; anon they pause,
Till Dionysus, from his car descending,
Tipsily leaned on one who may have been
That swart and swollen comrade, old Silenus,
Fain to enfold the yielding and flushed form,
Even as when the god wooed Ariadne;
So one may see them on a vase, or gem."

In Dionysos we find combined a beauty that can be as attractive to men as to women and the continued suggestion that he may happily be lover to either – or both.

Strangely, the god's potential role as a gay icon has never been exploited to the extent that one might have expected, having considered the classical myths. This is probably because (as I have discussed elsewhere) the great god Pan came to occupy this role in late Victorian and Edwardian English culture.[64] Dionysos' fluid sexuality wasn't wholly ignored, all the same. The sexual rights campaigner Edward Carpenter observed that:

> "Dionysus, one of the most remarkable figures in the Greek Mythology, is frequently represented as androgyne. Euripides in his *Bacchae* calls him 'feminine-formed' (*thelumorphos*), and the Orphic hymns 'double-sexed' (*diphues*); and Aristides in his discourse on Dionysus says: 'Thus the God is both male and female. His form corresponds to his nature, since everywhere in himself he is like a double being; for among young men he is a maiden, and among maidens a young man, and among men a beardless youth overflowing with vitality.'... 'In legend and art,' says Dr Frazer, 'there are clear traces of an effeminate Dionysus, and in some of his rites and processions men wore female attire.'"

Later in the same book, Carpenter daringly proposed that "those early figures – who once probably were men – those Apollos, Buddhas, Dionysus, Osiris, and so forth... were somewhat bi-sexual in temperament, and that it was really largely owing to that fact that they were endowed with far-reaching powers and became leaders of mankind."[65]

Despite being a Church of England vicar, Robert Herrick could be surprisingly erotic in his verse, as his poem *The Vine* demonstrates in startling but amusing terms:

64 See my *Great God Pan*, Green Magic, 2021.

65 Carpenter, *Intermediate Types among Primitive Folk*, 1914, 78 & 83.

"I dreamed this mortal part of mine
Was metamorphosed to a vine,
Which, crawling one and every way,
Enthralled my dainty Lucia.
Methought, her long small legs and thighs
I with my tendrils did surprise:
Her belly, buttocks, and her waist
By my soft nervelets were embraced
About her head I writhing hung
And with rich clusters (hid among
The leaves) her temples I behung,
So that my Lucia seemed to me
Young Bacchus ravished by his tree.
My curls about her neck did crawl,
And arms and hands they did enthrall,
So that she could not freely stir
(All parts therc made one prisoner).
But when I crept with leaves to hide
Those parts which maids keep unespied,
Such fleeting pleasures there I took
That with the fancy I awoke,
And found (ah me!) this flesh of mine
More like a stock than like a vine."

Fortunately for Herrick, then, wine could both stoke as well as quench desire…

MODERN MUSIC

Whilst the treatment of classical themes in poetry may come as little surprise, references in contemporary rock music to Dionysos may seem rather more improbable. Nevertheless, he is not entirely a stranger to stadium stages.

Canadian rock band Rush described the god as 'Dionysus bringer of love' on their 1970 album, *Hemispheres.* The deity promises "solace/In the darkness of the night," laughter, joy and the soothing of primal fears. He also offers liberation: "Throw off those chains of reason/And your prison disappears." The result is the heaven on earth that the cult has aimed for over millennia:

"The cities were abandoned,
And the forests echoed song;
They danced and lived as brothers
They knew love could not be wrong
Food and wine they had aplenty
And they slept beneath the stars..."

However, there's a sting in the tail to this contentment, because "winter fell upon them/And it caught them unprepared." Plainly, Rush were cynical about the god's message of love and unity. Modern heavy metal bands have chosen instead to emphasise the sexual aspects of the god. The Norwegian avant-garde black metal band *Solefald* identify Dionysos as the god of wine and ecstasy. They celebrate a spring feast with satyrs and bacchantes, to which a lover is invited:

"Undress to the sound of carcassing chorals
'Dionysify this night of spring,' Dionysified they sing.
The Aphrodite Loveroom glows with ruby walls
I gently tie you up in a bondage so mild
Your eyes float in the sea of red Bordeaux wine
I kiss you all over, passion-blind...
I tenderly adore the taste of your she
In this cathedral of cinnamon and sodomy..."[66]

66 *In Harmonia Universali*, 2003.

Polish extreme metal band *Behemoth* started to stray even further beyond myth and tradition in their visions of Dionysos. On the track *Daimonos,* on their album *Evangelion*, released in 2009, they called on the rulers of Sodom, the people of Gomorrah, and Chaldean priests to worship "the slain and risen God – All hail Dionysus…". This resurrected divinity is "various named, bull-faced/Begot from the thunder, Bacchus famed," which is all pretty authentic, but he is purely a god "of universal might, [of] swords and blood and sacred rage." The same band's *Starspawn* on the *Satanica* album from 1999 was rather more in line with Dionysos' nature, even echoing Rush: "everyone a star hath become/My brothers and sisters in cosmic ecstasy… We could make love to numberless stars…" This is the process of absorption in the god, of 'enthusiasm.' There may even be a touch of Crowley in this lyric, for he had a vision of the cosmos as a "star sponge" or as a "Nothingness with Twinkles" in which all thought and being were united, during the summer of 1916. A central concept of Crowley's *Thelema* was that "every man and woman is a star," entitled to an absolute right of self-fulfilment and expression.[67]

Other metal bands also exploit and develop the accepted vision of the god as a bringer of pleasure and physical passion. 'The Arcane Light of Hecate,' a song by the black metal group *Necromantia*, on their album *Scarlet Evil Witching Black*, released in 1995, is addressed to the queen of the witches, beseeching her to rise from the tomb so that she can "join the dance in the garden of Dionysus' delight/Joy of life (ecstasy of lust)/We embrace thy shining light tonight." *Necromantia* were, appropriately, from Athens; their song envisaged the dead being resurrected by Dionysos to enjoy the delights of the flesh.

In 1997 the Polish avant-garde metal band *Lux Occulta* released a whole album devoted to the "bull-horned god" *Dionysos*. The entire concept indicates a familiarity with the god and his cult. The tracks include 'Nocturnal Dithyramb' (the form

67 Booth, *A Magick Life*, 185.

of ancient Greek poem recited for the god – see Part One) and 'Ecstasy & Terror' which calls on the god to return and rule as king, although traditional aspects of his character are fused with something more violent and bloodthirsty (as was also the case with their later compatriots *Behemoth*):

> "Hail Zagreus! Hail Bromios! Let the Great Hunt begin ...
> His golden hair streams in the wind
> As he spills the blood of his enemies
> Be thou our king!
> Delight of Mortals, The One Who Breaks the Chains – Gloria!
> God of Many Joys, Giver of Wine – Gloria!
> Lord of Souls, Eater of Raw Flesh – Gloria!
> The One Who Changes his Forms – Gloria!
> The One Who Delights in Sword and Bloodshed – Gloria!
> Prince of Daylight and the Underworld Darkness – Gloria!"

On a lighter note, English pagan goths *Inkubus Sukkubus* were quite blatant about the god's links with alcohol and fun. Their song 'Jägermeister,' on *The Beast with Two Backs* (2004), is about the popular liqueur of that name: it's "Heaven's milk... Mana from the stars above/The liquid flame of fire and shame." This "liquid gold" is, in fact, the "sweetest blood from the veins of Pan" and Bacchus and Dionysus are both called upon to "lead me up to the lips of Isis," from despair to ecstasy.

In 2006, American band the *Orion Experience* released the album *Cosmicandy* which included a pop rock song titled 'Cult of Dionysus.' The track imagines a couple deciding to start a new religion as a means of rediscovering the joy and excitement in their lives. The resulting cult exploits many of the Bacchanalian tropes first propagated by Livy, with some measure of Crowley thrown in:

"Yeah, we're gonna build a temple to our love
Orgiastic dances, nymphs in trances
Yeah, we'll be the envy of the gods above
I'm feeling devious
You're looking glamorous
Let's get mischievous
And polyamorous
Wine and women and wonderful vices
Welcome to the cult of Dionysus.

We could take a holiday in the month of May
Run free and play in fields of flowers
Pass the hours making love is how we'll pray,
Or start a secret society for the wild and free
Our ideology is "You can do what you want
Too much is never enough"
We are the life, we are the light..."

The aim is to escape the world and its tears, to reject war, pain, waste and greed by propagating a message of love and hope that favours of indulgence and ecstasy. The jolly, sing-along track certainly does a good job of promoting the new cult.

Long-running Australian musical project *Dead Can Dance* in 2018 released a short album titled *Dionysus*. Founder member Brendan Perry described the inspiration as being a trance-like, Dionysian experience he had at a Spanish festival. He was convinced that such rural spring celebrations represent the modern survivals of Dionysian rites: "People wear masks and dance in circles, almost like time has stood still in their celebrations."

The result was a 'two-act' record that represents "different facets of the Dionysus myth and his cult." The music is divided across seven tracks, each intended to portray a new aspect of the god's story. Traditional folk instruments such as balalaika and bagpipes are employed and the vocals are written in an invented tongue, what vocalist Lisa Gerrard has called "the language of the heart." The album tracks are suitably titled, including *Invocation, Liberation of Minds* and *Dance of the Bacchantes.* The latter is a pulsing, driving combination of percussion, pipes, strings and wordless vocals, perfectly fitted to the gyrations of the bacchae.

MODERN THEATRE

Euripides' *Bacchae* has been handled by classical musicians numerous times: Holst set part of it in the 'Hymn to Dionysus' of 1913; Philip Glass has also scored the play and there have been at least half a dozen operatic versions. One, *The Bassarids* (1966), was scored by Hans Werner Henze with a libretto by W.H. Auden.

The play itself has been staged multiple times over the last half century, for example as *Erpingham Camp* by Joe Orton in 1966, as *A Communion Rite* by Wole Soyinka in 1973, by Ingmar Bergman at the Royal Dramatic Theatre, Stockholm, in 1996 (one of three versions with which he was involved) and in a National Theatre of Scotland rock and roll version in 2007 which starred Alan Cumming as the young god. There have been several television and film versions, too: for example, by Brian de Palma in 1969, by Ingmar Bergman (1993) and, most recently, in 2002 by Brad Mays.

Stephen Sondheim and Burt Shevelove in 1974 adapted Aristophanes' comedy *The Frogs* into a modern musical. The stage-play retained the descent of Dionysos into Hades to bring back a playwright; however, the writers were updated, with Dionysos having to choose between George Bernard Shaw and William Shakespeare.

Earlier, we examined R.C. Trevelyan's *Bride of Dionysus.* This text was used as the libretto for an opera by the composer Donald Tovey. Written between 1907 and 1913, it was first performed in Edinburgh in 1929, with stage designs by the artist Charles Ricketts (for whom see later). Neither Dionysos, his entourage nor his story remain hidden from us for long.

Dionysos' Followers in Modern Culture

"And dance when Dionysus beats his gong:"[68]

Much poetic inspiration has been derived from the Dionysos-Bacchus and his gift of wine, but equal (and possibly growing) attention has been directed to his followers, and their behaviour. They create a communal feel that is both companionable as well as helping to generate the sense of ecstasy.

Seventeenth century poet Thomas Heywood, for instance, portrayed the music and movement that was an essential element in the overall transporting feeling of the Dionysian rites:

"The Satyres, and goat-footed Aegipines,
Will with their rurall musicke come and meete thee,
With boxen pypes, and countrey Tamburines,
Faunus and olde Sylvanus, they will greete thee.
Then leave not them, which seem thus to admire thee,
And leave not her, that doeth so sore desire thee." [69]

Perceptions had changed very little a century and a half later; John Keats was steeped in the classical myths and understood their vitality and power keenly, as his *Endymion,* composed in 1817, demonstrates very well. He imagined meeting Dionysos and his *thiasos:*

"Twas Bacchus and his crew!
The earnest trumpet spake, and silver thrills
From kissing cymbals made a merry din-

68 James Elroy Flecker, *The Bridge of Fire,* 1907.
69 Heywood, from *Oenone & Paris*, 1594.

'Twas Bacchus and his kin!
Like to a moving vintage down they came,
Crown'd with green leaves, and faces all on flame;
All madly dancing through the pleasant valley,
To scare thee, Melancholy!"

In his verse, Keats addresses the satyrs and the maenads and is invited to join their "wild minstrelsy." The satyrs frankly declare that "For wine we follow Bacchus through the earth/Great God of breathless cups and chirping mirth!" whilst the women reply to his enquiries:

"Whence came ye, merry Damsels! whence came ye!
So many, and so many, and such glee?
Why have ye left your bowers desolate,
Your lutes, and gentler fate?'
'We follow Bacchus! Bacchus on the wing,
A-conquering!
Bacchus, young Bacchus! good or ill betide,
We dance before him thorough kingdoms wide…'"[70]

There's exhilaration, devotion and – naturally – free drink to lure followers to go along.

The story of Bacchus and Ariadne enabled poets to portray the god as the rescuing hero and ideal lover, coming to save the abandoned and lonely girl with all the excitement and clamour of his entourage. Here is Leigh Hunt's vision:

"Suddenly from a wood his dancers rush.
Leaping like wines that from the bottle gush;
Bounding they come, and twirl, and thrust on high
Their thyrsoses, as they would rouse the sky;
And hurry here and there, in loosened bands,

70 Keats, *Endymion*, Part IV, lines 196–236.

And trill above their heads their cymballed hands:
Some, brawny males, that almost show from far
Their forceful arms, cloudy and muscular;
Some, smoother females, who have nevertheless
Strong limbs, and hands, to fling with and to press;
And shapes, which they can bend with heavenward glare.
And tortuous wrists, and backward streaming hair.
A troop of goat-foot shapes came trampling after.
Bacchus took in his arms his bridal lass.
And gave and shared as much more happiness
Then Theseus, as a noble spirit's caress.
Full of sincerity, and mind, and heart."[71]

In *Atalanta in Calydon* (1865), Algernon Charles Swinburne very effectively evoked the more sexual thrill of involvement in Dionysos' retinue, an element that had, perhaps, hitherto been more implicit in much of the poetry:

"And Pan by noon and Bacchus by night,
Fleeter of foot than the fleet-foot kid,
Follows with dancing and fills with delight
The Maenad and the Bassarid;
And soft as lips that laugh and hide
The laughing leaves of the trees divide,
And screen from seeing and leave in sight
The god pursuing, the maiden hid.
The ivy falls with the Bacchanal's hair
Over her eyebrows hiding her eyes;
The wild vine slipping down leaves bare
Her bright breast shortening into sighs…"

Indeed, some of this passionate emotion seems to have been a response to the handsome young god himself:

---

71 James Henry Leigh Hunt, *Bacchus & Ariadne*, lines 339–342.

"Or such darkest ivy-buds
As divide thy yellow hair,
Bacchus, and their leaves that nod
Round thy fawnskin brush the bare
Snow-soft shoulders of a god..."[72]

Only a few years later, British novelist, playwright and poet James Elroy Flecker (1884–1915) imagined how the arrival of Bacchus might affect Edwardian London:

"From Heaven's Gate to Hampstead Heath
Young Bacchus and his crew
Came tumbling down, and o'er the town
Their bursting trumpets blew..."

All of London society, from the king down to busmen flocked to see "The God and all his crew/Silenus pulled by nymphs, a faun/ A satyr drenched in dew" and learned to rejoice – all except for Parliament, where all the members remained steadfastly asleep.[73]

The God of Women

The understanding persists that Dionysos is, above all, a deity associated with the female. Walter Pater wrote that the bassarids were the divinity's true sisters, clad like him in the long dress-like tunic called the *bassara*. Dionysos therefore was "himself a woman-like god" and so:

"it was on women and feminine souls that his power mainly fell. At Elis, it was the women who had their own little song with which at spring-time they professed to call him from the sea: at Brasiae they had their own temple where none

72 Swinburne, *Atalanta in Calydon*, choruses to 'When the hounds of Spring' & 'O that I now.'
73 Flecker, *The Ballad of Hampstead Heath*.

> but women might enter; and so the thiasus, also, is almost exclusively formed of women – of those who experience most directly the influence of things which touch thought through the senses – the presence of night, the expectation of morning, the nearness of wild, unsophisticated, natural things – the echoes, the coolness, the noise of frightened creatures as they climbed through the darkness, the sunrise seen from the hill-tops, the disillusion, the bitterness of satiety, the deep slumber which comes with the morning."

In these women's rites there survived more ancient religious customs, "an enthusiasm otherwise relegated to the wonderland of a distant past, in which a supposed primitive harmony and understanding between man and nature renewed itself."[74]

Bacchantes & Bassarids

As we have already seen, the Greeks considered the followers of the god to be loose women – this was both their shame *and* their attraction. Poets have perpetuated and reinforced this image down the centuries. In Elizabethan times Thomas Nashe made a telling comparison, "Like a franticke Bacchinall, she stampt" and Shakespeare invoked "The ryot of the tipsie Bachanals." Spirited and independent women had a powerful allure for men.[75]

In 1705, George Stanhope's *A paraphrase and comment upon the epistles and gospels, appointed to be used in the Church of England* predictably took a dim view of the fact that "Intemperance and Excess in the Heathen Bacchanals was esteemed an Act of religious Joy." For many, though, this was not a fault but a powerful attraction: the supplement to *Chambers' Cyclopaedia* of 1753 defined 'bacchanalia/bacchanals' as "pictures or basso relievos, whereon the feast is represented, consisting chiefly

74 Pater, *Greek Studies*, 57–58 & 64.

75 Nashe, *The Unfortunate Traveller*, 1594, sig. N4; Shakespeare, *Midsummer Night's Dream*, 1600, Act 5 scene 1.

of dancings, nudities, and the like." Horace Walpole *Vertue's Anecdotes* of 1763 only reinforced such perceptions, describing, for example, "A Bacchanal of naked boys, sitting on a tub, the wine running out."[76]

The message from antiquity seemed clear: bacchanals and bacchantes were fun. Thomas Holcroft in 1797 described a woman who "capered with the intoxication of a Bacchante." Thomas Moore's translation of Anacreon excited readers with thoughts of "Many a rose-lipped bacchant maid… culling clusters in their shade" and, in 1818, Byron heard "The bacchanal roar of the songs of exultation."[77]

Very little has altered in more recent times. Shelley had mentioned "some fierce maenad" in his *Ode to the West Wind* and the lure of a wild but willing partner remains just as strong- as Ernest Dowson knew very well:

> "Ah, Manon, say!
> Expound, I pray, the mystery
> Why wine-stained lip and languid eye,
> And most unsaintly Maenad air,
> Should move us more than all the rare
> White roses of virginity?"[78]

Ezra Pound was later to observe of Dowson that he "found harlots cheaper than hotels."[79] Charles-Pierre Baudelaire had envisioned maenads in very much the same way. The poem 'Femmes Damnées' (Damned Women) in his 1857 collection, *Les Fleurs du Mal,* is unforgivingly scathing. These women, with their "purple bare breasts of temptations" are "demons, monsters, martyrs all."

---

76 Stanhope, *Paraphrase*, Book 3, 544; Walpole, *Anecdotes*, Painting III, 1, 18.

77 Holcroft, translation of F.L. Stolberg *Travels through Germany*, 1797, Book III, c.77,170; Moore, *Anacreon Odes*, 1800, iv, 15; Byron, *Childe Harold*, Canto IV Dedication, xii.

78 Dowson, *Rondeau.*

79 Ezra Pound, *Sienna mi fe.*

"Some of them, in the light of torches wan,
In silent hollow caves, pagan retreats,
Ask you for help in their delirium,
O Bacchus, who can lull the old regrets."

The poet was at once fascinated and repelled: "I both love and pity you" he declared to these women with their 'insatiable thirsts.' Amongst Baudelaire's censored poems that were published in 1866, there was second with exactly the same title as that in *Les Fleurs*. This concerns two women called Delphine and Hippolyta who are lovers; it seems that their forbidden ardour for each other is what has condemned them: Hippolyta indeed asks her partner "Avons-nous donc commis une action étrange?" (Have we done a terrible thing?). Their desire for each other is insatiable, an indication that Baudelaire (at least) was simultaneously intrigued but alarmed by unbridled female passion- by feminine desire that stood outside the boundaries and controls of a male world.

The Irish poet Edward Power (1951–2019) also conjured this sense (from the male perspective) of the dangerous sexuality of the bacchante. His *Maenad* has "Something unspeakable/ In the almonds of her eyes." She has a threatening fertility:

"The Maenad straddles ocean.
Soon will break white horses
From the swell of her vulva,
Sting of her laughter."

She's a fusion of a Sheela-na-gig figure and a mermaid and we're warned that "Later/When stars come naked/From the hiding-place of creation/She'll rape a jellyfish."[80]

In the middle of the next century, American poet (and translator of Baudelaire) Clark Ashton Smith showed himself

80 *Poetry Ireland Review*, 2021, issue 24, page 37.

fully aware of the same allure. In *Bacchante* he addressed a woman who had been able to reconnect him with "the ancient madness and the ancient glory," so that it did not feel as if the "gods have flown/[or that] the Golden Age is but a fading story." Rather:

> "Under the thyrse upholden,
> We have felt the thrilling presence of the god,
> And you, Bacchante, shod
> With moonfire, and with moonfire all enfolden,
> Have danced upon the mystery-haunted sod.
> With every autumn blossom,
> And with the brown and verdant leaves of vine,
> We have filled your hair divine;
> From the cupped hollow of your delicious bosom
> We have drunk wine, Bacchante, purple wine."

In the moonlight, this "dancer of our delight" has been able to conjure up "Maenad and Bassarid in spectral rout." Somehow, in her dancing form she has embodied a "magic urn/Wherefrom is poured the pagan gramarie" making the watchers' "bardic blood and spirit burn/[with] dreams and fevers of antiquity."

R.C. Trevelyan tried to capture some sense of the demented ecstasy of the young god's followers:

> "Where the Maenads ivy-cinctured toss their heads back vehemently.
> Where they shake the holy emblems with shrill ululating cries,
> Where that roving rout of the Goddess to and fro is wont to flit.
> Whither now 'tis meet for us too to be whirled in a rapid dance."[81]

81 R.C. Trevelyan, *The Attys of Catullus*.

The prolific American nature poet Madison Julius Cawein (1865–1914) several times described maenads and bacchic ecstasies. Additionally, this poet's natural imagery was always heavily loaded with classical and supernatural characters and images, as well as frequently being highly sensual. His poem *Forest and Field* is no exception to this; for example, flies are:

> "Like drops of amber-scattered wine
> Spun high by reeling Bacchanals,
> When Bacchus wreathes his curling hair
> With vine-leaves, and from every lair
> His worshippers around him calls."

Cawein's poem *Dionysia* lives up to its name, too. One night the poet hears sounds in a nearby dell and discovers there a woman:

> "Mænad, Bassarid, Bacchant,
> What you will, who doth enchant
> Night with sensuous nudity.
> Lo! again I hear her pant
> Breasting through the dewy glooms."

This woman is then depicted in sensuous and highly erotic terms, before the poet joins her:[82]

> "In the mad and Mænad dance
> Onward dragged with violence;
> Pan and old Silenus and
> Faunus and a Bacchant band
> Round me. Wild my wine-stained hand
> O'er tumultuous hair is lifted;
> While the flushed and Phallic orgies

82 Similar ecstatic descriptions of a lover are also found Cawein's Dionysian poem *Dithyrambics*.

Whirl around me; and the marges
Of the wood are torn and rifted
With lascivious laugh and shout.
And barbarian there again,
Shameless with the shameless rout,
Bacchus lusting in each vein,
With her pagan lips on mine,
Like a god made drunk with wine,
On I reel; and, in the revels,
Her loose hair, the dance dishevels,
Blows, and 'thwart my vision swims
All the splendour of her limbs..."

Similar terms are used by Cawein when recounting the bacchanal seen by him during a dream, which began with a visit from a maenad. The reborn god then appeared in his leopard-drawn chariot to the sound of pipes and cymbals; there were wild dances and wine – the "Bacchanalian draught/Spun from the giddy bowl, a rose-tinged mist." Cawein experienced the "strangeness of the orgies wildly cried" and then begged the god for death, having hymned his triumph.[83]

Interestingly too, rather like Francis Joseph Sherman, whose comparison of Bacchus to a bee we noticed earlier, Cawein used very similar insect metaphors for the god's entourage: "the bee/ All honey-drunk, a Bassarid" and "Silenus-like, eyes stolidly/The Mænad-glittering dragonfly."[84]

Francis Bret Harte (1836-1902) described too delirious maenads, bassarids and bacchantes gambolling and singing "free-eyed." In another poem, Madison Cawein depicted a woman sitting on the steps of a shrine of Dionysos, beautiful but dishevelled and exhausted by the god's devotions:

83 Cawein, *Dionysos*.
84 Cawein, *Forest & Field*.

"A priest of Bacchus passed, nor stopped
To chide her; deeming her whose chiton hid
But half her bosom, and whose girdle dropped,
Some grief-drowned Bassarid,
The god of wine had chid."

The overwhelming emotions of the god's frenzy can leave the maenads almost heedless of themselves and unaware of danger or fear – so that neither the presence of snakes nor big cats can perturb them.[85]

The special status of maenads as women who – at least for a while – stand outside societal and behavioural norms, has attracted many poets, especially women. Sylvia Plath (1932–63) was one writer who was alive to this. For her twenty-seventh birthday in October 1959, she wrote the poem *Maenad,* in which she examined this weird difference and separateness. The first line, "Once I was ordinary" established the tone. Plath continued "I am too big to go backward;" she doesn't feel able to be reborn, but time continues to unwind like an umbilical cord. During the autumn "the dead ripen in the grapeleaves," and she asks to be fed "the berries of dark," perhaps so that she can join them and rise again in spring.

It seems that modern poet Ursula K. Le Guin (1929–2018) understood not only the sacred nature of these women's raptures and frenzies, but their potential vulnerability to hostile men and the fact that their holiness had to be preserved. She refers in her poem *Maenads* to story of the women of Amphissa, an incident related earlier in Part One. After their frenzy on the mountain was over, the women descended to the nearest town-

"... past drunk,
hoarse, half naked, blear-eyed,

85 F. Bret Harte, *The Lost Tails of Miletus*; Cawein, *Before the Temple*; Ezra Pound, *Canto LXXIX.*

blood dried under broken nails
and across young thighs,
but still jeering and joking, still trying
to dance, lurching and yelling, but falling
dead asleep by the market stalls…"

Unable to look after each other like this, being sprawled flat out and helpless, local women – middle-aged, respectable housewives, came to safeguard them, standing-

"night-long in the agora
silent
together…
guarding, watching them
as their mothers
watched over them.
And no man
dared
that fierce decorum."

As we shall see later, this scene was also depicted by the renowned painter Lawrence Alma-Tadema. Scared as many men might be of the maenads at the height of their fury, when they manifest their full awesome divinely inspired power, when they are wantonly unconscious, it may be another matter. Then their position outside social convention may offer them no protection and, in fact, their 'loose' reputation may actively endanger them. It is at this point that another community of women steps in to protect what is valuable and admirable in their society. Le Guin understood that the 'mothering' instinct was triggered by an appreciation of what was felt to have meaning and importance- the maenads' shared mystical encounter. The women were neighbours, parents and relatives, but they had gone out to the mountains and had contacted the divine. When they returned home, to live once more as family and friends, they brought their experience of sanctity into their daily relationships. They had been transformed and, in turn, they might change those around them.

Lastly, the ecstasy of the maenads in the presence of the god should not make us neglect the relevance of other aspects of Dionysos' character to his female followers. The American poet Eunice Tietjens (1844–1944) deftly indicates this in her 1915 poem *The Bacchante to her Babe.* The birth of the child is part of the process of renewal of the natural world which the deity oversees. The mother calls on her child join her now in her dances and to be:

> "Glad with all the procreant earth,
> With all the fruitage of the trees,
> And golden pollen on the breeze,
> With plants that bring the grain to birth."

Ultimately, of course, the mother understands that "we are part of all, we two/For my glad burgeoning in you!" In childbearing, just as much as in her trances, she partakes of the rebirth that Dionysos represents.

Maenads in Music

Many contemporary rock bands have taken up the maenad as the symbol of the original and ultimate 'riot girl.' Bacchantes are consistently seen as physically and mentally frenzied. *Apollo Makes Fire,* a psychedelic rock band from Ohio, rank dancing daemons and maenads together in their song 'Storm of a Thousand Winds.' Swedish symphonic metal band *Therion,* on their track 'From the Dionysus Days,' call upon Pan to provide the music and

> "make all the Bacchants gather in Arcady
> To dance on the Festival of the Tragedy
> And eat the fruits of ecstasy."[86]

For very many present-day bands, the manic passion of the bacchantes would appear to be wholly inseparable from alcohol and from sex. For example, Greek *Trio Tekke* praise the "wizard wine" and call to a potential lover:

> "My lady, you have a place in my blaze-
> Heat of the depths, lust, burns and pain;
> Slip into my arms, you flushed maenad,
> Let's groan the night together
> like hungry wolves."[87]

Spanish folk metal band *Theratos* likewise understood that both wine and women were central to any truly abandoned celebration of Bacchus:

> "Maenads, music, flutes and harps
> Two times born and both quite drunk
> Hail the god of wine and lust..."[88]

We encountered Polish metal band *Lux Occulta* a littler earlier. On the album named in his honour, Dionysos is envisaged returning to earth accompanied by lustful satyrs making "Women that hunger for life open wide their tender treasuries" ('Blessed Be the Rain'). Sex is regarded as a sacrament to the god; the

86 *Therion*, from the album *Crowning of Atlantis*, 1997. 'Therion' is, by the way, the Greek for 'beast' and was one of Crowley's names for himself.

87 *Trio Tekke*, 'Shooting Star' on *Strovilos*, 2020.

88 *Theratos*, song 'Blacklips', on *Dionysus Warlords*, 2021; see too 'Faceless' by *aka Funeral* or *Virgin Steele*'s 'Green Dusk Blues' on 2018's *Ghost Harvest, Theatre of Tragedy*'s 'Bacchante' (1998) and *Züül*'s 'Fist First.' This last is as explicit as it sounds, although without the lyric sheet you'd probably not get a word of the vocals and would miss the reference to 'bacchae.'

song 'Chalice of Lunar Blood' imagines coupling with a snake- and ivy-wreathed queen and 'Nocturnal Dithyramb' depicts ecstatic dances with a "lion-woman." This imagery culminates on the track 'Ecstasy and Terror,' which gives a central role to the maenads in the cult of the god, evoking a sensuous and violent sexuality:

> "Aroused women wash their naked bodies
> In bubbling springs of sweet dark wine;
> The whole world will dance in this joyful time
> Everything blossoms, even the stones sing dithyrambs.
> His golden hair streams in the wind
> As he dances with the nymphs…
> Maenads – his hunting dogs – are now unleashed,
> Frenzied women devour their crying children
> Phalli carved out of stone plough cold, dead wombs"

Sex is never far away with the bacchae, perhaps most surprisingly in the song 'Chateau Interieur' (Interior Castle) by Breton avant-garde singer Brigitte Fontaine (b.1939). Its lyrics are particularly explicit – as well as being bizarrely at odds with both the traditional French *chanson* backing and with the original source of the title, which is a spiritual development guide written by St Theresa of Avila in 1577:

> "In the orgies room
> Weep the candlesticks
> On polished bellies,
> On the fire of necklaces.
>
> The come and the sweat
> Bathe in the silk of the sheets;
> Burning lights,
> Golden niagaras.

> Lesbians and bacchantes
> Stick fairies and priapics
> In the wicked fury
> Of their dances in clusters…"[89]

Erotic Ecstasies – Pierre Louys

The modern perception of the bacchantes as highly sexual beings has just been seen. The sexual nature of the Dionysian rites was discussed earlier and, as we saw, the ancient Greek celebrations of the god seem to have involved same sex practices just as much as heterosexual. We may recall Dionysos and the wooden dildo he fashioned in memory of the man Prosymnus. We may also remember the 'secret objects' used during the Dionysian mysteries – these appear to have included a fig-wood phallus that was revealed to new followers as part of their initiation.

In his ground-breaking book, the *Songs of Bilitis*, published in 1894, Belgian author Pierre Louys imaginatively and freely described some of the ecstatic ceremonies performed for the divine lovers, Dionysus and Aphrodite:

> "Through the forests that overhang the sea, the maenads madly rushed. Maskale, with the hot breasts, howled and brandished the sycamore phallos, smeared with red. All leaped and ran and cried aloud beneath their robes and crowns of twisted vine, crotals clacking in their hands, and thyrses splitting the bursting skins of echoing dulcimers. With sopping hair and agile limbs, breasts reddened and tossed about, sweat of cheeks and foam of lips, oh, Dionysos! they offered in return the love that you had poured in them. And the sea-wind tossed Heliokomis' russet hair unto the sky, and whipped it into a furious flame on her body's white-wax torch."

89 On the album *Libido*, 2006.

> "I shall reveal a portion of the rite, but no more of it than is permitted. About a crowned Phallus, a hundred and twenty women swayed and cried. The initiates were dressed as men, the others in the split tunics. The fumes of incense and the smoke of torches floated like clouds around us. I wept burning tears and then… we threw all ourselves down, stretched on our backs. Then, when the religious act had been consummated, and when into the holy triangle the purpled phallus had been plunged anew, the mysteries began; but I shall say no more."[90]

Elsewhere in *Bilitis,* Louys depicted a scene in which a woman visits Bilitis and her girlfriend to ask to borrow an 'object' as this neighbour is planning to see her own lover, Myrrhina, whom she describes as little, pretty and lascivious.[91]

Louys seems to have done his research on ancient Greek culture and to have understood perfectly well what went on. It seems very likely that he took up the suggestion about the bacchantes from sources such as *The Bacchae.* Furthermore, one of the sapphic rites in his book *Aphrodite* ends with a death, a parallel perhaps to the sacrifices of the Dionysian frenzies.[92]

Louys imagined rites as scandalous as anything that ancient historians such as Livy had hinted at so disapprovingly. Worked into a frenzy by wine and dance, the young god's worshippers all have sex in turn with a woman wearing a wooden dildo, re-enacting the union of the divine couple Dionysos and Aphrodite/Astarte. Predictably for this particular author, he placed sex – and especially lesbian sex – at the heart of the rites. It is not clear how historically accurate this really was, but it reflected – and doubtless helped to shape – the developing ideas about Dionysian orgies that remain with us today.

---

90 Louys, *Songs* 64–67.
91 *Bilitis*, Song 75.
92 See too my *Aphrodite – Goddess of Modern Love*, Green Magic, 2021.

It remains to observe that Louys was not the only one who detected these pansexual undercurrents to the maenads. The American poet Blanche Shoemaker Wagstaff (1888–1867) wrote the remarkable 'Bacchante' in 1918 for her collection *Narcissus:*

> "I am inebriate with the sunlight's golden wine,
> And I would love with an insensate fury!
>
> Let me drain beauty even unto death!
> Bring me a languid woman, perfumed, young,
> Her dusky body hung with dazzling gems
> And strange exotic iridescent stuffs-
> Her wanton eyes like thirsty summer moons.
>
> Oh, I would love with an insensate fury!
> Bring me a pale flower-boy,
> White-limbed like a young heifer in a field,
> His lips aquiver with unknown desire ...
> His soft throat virgin beneath my kiss,
> His bosom like a bower of stars.
>
> I would dance like a drunken fawn amid the wood,
> Enraptured with the budding pollen-scents!"

Pierre Louys' erotic vision of the Dionysian rites was not his only treatment of the god's cult. In his short story *Ariadne*, published during the 1890s, he presented a unique interpretation of the story of the Minoan princess and of the nature of the god.[93]

Having been abandoned by Theseus on Naxos, Ariadne awakes to sound of bacchantes, satyrs and pans approaching. The maenads are described vividly: "Their hands waved branches of trees and shook garlands of ivy. Their hair was so laden with

93 *Ariadne* was published separately, but will generally now be found collected with other short related stories as *The Twilight of the Nymphs*.

flowers that their necks bent backward; the folds of their breasts were rivulets of sweat, their thighs glowed like setting suns and their shrieks were spotted with flying foam." They cry out to Iacchos – "Beautiful God! Mighty God! Living God! Leader of the Orgy!" imploring him to "Incite the multitude! Drive the rout and the rapid feet! We are yours! We are your swelling breath! We are your turbulent desires!"

As soon as the frenzied women see Ariadne, they tear her limp from limb and scatter her remains. Dionysos then appears, dismisses them, and resurrects their victim, intoning over her dismembered corpse "Arise! I am Awakening. I am Life. This is the road of Eternal Peace."

Then, rather than marrying Ariadne, as the traditional story tells, this Dionysos makes her his queen, of a place "where you shall never again see the sun too glittering not the night too shadowy… you shall never again feel hunger nor thirst nor love nor fatigue…" He is the "Ruler of Shades, the Master of the Infernal Water" and she shall sit beside him on his throne presiding over a land where "the anguish of death is miraculously transfigured in the intoxication of resurrection," where pain and trouble become ecstatic and where a great eternal peace reigns. Ariadne is overjoyed with this prospect – and then he annihilates her completely.

Again, Louys has evidently undertaken his research and has chosen to explore the strand of the ancient myth that made Dionysos an equivalent of Hades/Pluto and lord of the underworld (see Part One). It is a uniquely bleak and savage conception of the god, but certainly not one without classical authority.

Picturing the God

How we envisage Dionysos is shaped as much by his representation in art as it is by literature. We have inherited a rich iconography from classical times, which is naturally reflective of the complex mythology and symbolism associated with the god. Walter Pater declared that – whatever the religious symbolism of the cult of Dionysos, "certainly, for art, and a poetry delighting in colour and form, it was a custom rich in suggestion. The imitative arts would draw from it altogether new motives of freedom and energy, of freshness in old forms. It is from this fantastic scene that the beautiful wind-touched draperies, the rhythm, the heads suddenly thrown back, of many a Pompeian wall-painting and sarcophagus-frieze are originally derived; and that melting languor, that perfectly composed lassitude of the fallen Maenad, became a fixed type in the school of grace, the school of Praxiteles."[94]

THE CLASSICAL LEGACY

Greek and Roman art established a standard way of depicting Dionysos and his followers. This was rediscovered during the Renaissance and has remained influential into the present.

Although the earliest images of Dionysos showed a mature male, bearded and robed and holding his thyrsos, he later came to be depicted as a beardless, sensuous, naked or half-naked androgynous youth: as we've already learned, too, the literature described him as womanly or even 'man-womanish.' It's in this younger, handsome form that he's best known to us today.

Another key image of the cult in ancient times was Dionysos returning triumphant from his conquests over places beyond

94 Pater, *Greek Studies*, 58–59.

the borders of the known and civilised world. His triumphal procession (*thiasos*) is made up of bearded satyrs with erect penises and his wild female followers, the maenads, wearing wreaths of ivy and with serpents coiled around their hair or necks. Some of these are armed with the thyrsos, some dance or play music.[95] The god himself is drawn in a chariot, usually by exotic beasts such as lions or tigers, and is sometimes attended by a bearded, drunken Silenus. This triumph is presumed to have provided the model for processions by his cult followers. Whilst the stories behind his triumphs may have become less familiar, the image of Bacchus in his chariot is one that was regularly painted since the Renaissance and remains familiar to many even today.

A number of attributes or accoutrements are commonly seen with Dionysos in the classical imagery, helping us to identify the deity we are looking at as well as suggesting key aspects of his story. The snake and phallus were symbols of Dionysos and Bacchus in Greece and Rome; he is said to have been crowned with snakes after his 'second' birth. Making friends with snakes was seen as a Dionysian trait. As a symbol, snakes have many meanings. They are phallic symbols but, at the same time, they were believed to be androgynous and so represented the fertility of the earth and the power of certain saviour deities to regenerate and resurrect themselves. What's more, when the baby Dionysos was set upon by the titans, he initially evaded their murderous assault by changing his form – from lion to horse to snake. So it is, then, that the god often appears in a chariot drawn by large ferocious felines, amongst which the golden leopardess (or panther) was most common; sometimes the god was shown actually riding the large cat. Dionysos might also wear a leopard skin over his shoulders. The cat seems to symbolise the deity's function as destroyer and creator, although one authority tells

95 It's worth noting that the *thiasos* retinue is something that Dionysos shares with only one other deity, Artemis.

us that "Dionysus is devoted to this animal because it is the most excitable of beasts and leaps lightly like a bacchante" whereas the writer Athenaeus had an interesting alternative explanation: "From the condition produced by wine they liken Dionysos to a bull or panther, because they who have indulged too freely are prone to violence... There are some drinkers who become full of rage like a bull... Others, though, become like wild beasts in their desire to fight, whence the likeness to a panther."[96]

Goats and rams are also linked with the god. As was mentioned at the start of Part One, this mainly seems to be related to the fraught relationship that prevails between wine-growers and grazing livestock, although there may well be sexual connotations to this link too.

As described earlier, the cult of Dionysos associated him closely with trees, so that he might be depicted with these, especially apples and figs. Vines and grapes were commonly present, most often as wreaths around the brows; from time to time, he might even appear dressed in a cloak made entirely of grapes. The vine symbolised resurrection, because its strength was preserved in the wine made from it.

Ivy was also frequently depicted, again most regularly in wreaths the god wore as well as twined around the thyrsos, as an ivy cup (*kantharos*) from which wine was drunk or as green shoots sprouting from a post. Ivy symbolises both immortality and revelry. According to Robert Graves, ivy was sacred to Osiris as well as to Dionysos; the poet also suggested that the bassarids, rather than drinking wine, got drunk on 'spruce ale' brewed from the sap of the silver fir and laced with ivy – or that they chewed ivy leaves to supplement their mushroom high. Wreaths of yew, oak and pine might also be worn.[97]

The thyrsos itself is typically specified to have been made from the hollow dried stem of a fennel. In itself, there seems little

96 Philostratus, *Imagines*, 1.19.1; Athenaeus, *Deipnosophistae*, 2.38e.

97 Graves, *White Goddess*, 183.

reason for favouring fennel over any other tall plant or – better still – a stick. However, it was a plant sacred to the Thracian sky god Sabazios, another deity with whom Dionysos was sometimes equated. Wreaths of fennel were worn at Sabazios' ceremonies, which may explain its present amongst Dionysos' attributes.

Dionysos is also closely associated with the transition between summer and autumn. Pindar describes the "pure light of high summer" as being linked with the god, possibly even being an embodiment of the deity himself. An ancient Greek image of Dionysos' birth from Zeus' thigh labels him "the light of Zeus" (*Dios phos*) and associates him with the light of Sirius.

As just noted, Dionysos often appears in sculptures and paintings and on pottery with figures representing his followers. Centaurs, fauns, satyrs, nymphs, Silenus, Pan and Hermaphrodite are commonly seen. It's also notable that sculpture of the late, 'Hellenistic' period started to include mortal subjects, such as of children and peasants, who might carry objects associated with the god's festivals such as ivy wreaths. The representation of his human devotees is a feature of more Dionysian modern art we shall examine in some detail in due course.

THE RENAISSANCE OF DIONYSOS

Bacchic subjects in art were taken up again quite late in the Renaissance in Italy, but they soon became almost as popular as in antiquity. The symbolism just described was inherited from the classical imagery, yet the artists appeared to have drawn upon a relatively limited set of literary sources. Perhaps this was in part due to the fact that Dionysos/Bacchus was not dealt with in any detail by some of the best-known writers – Ovid or Plato for example; perhaps, too, his adventures seemed less interesting. Whatever the exact reason, and despite the wide range of incidents and stories involved in the mythos of Dionysos, he was transmitted to later generations in a rather narrow form.

He appeared as the god of wine and drunken excess (endlessly); secondly, he appeared as the rescuer of Ariadne on Naxos. That may have been more to do with the fact that the incident formed a sequel to the far more popular story of Theseus and the minotaur, but it was, nonetheless, a charming love story and one that retained the same appeal it had in classical times:

> "For instance, the ivy clusters forming a crown are the clear mark of Dionysus, even if the workmanship is poor; and a horn just springing from the temples reveals Dionysus, and a leopard, though but just visible, is a symbol of the god; but this Dionysus the painter has characterized by love alone. Flowered garments and thyrsi and fawn-skins have been cast aside as out of place for the moment, and the Bacchantes are not clashing their cymbals now, nor are the Satyrs playing the flute, nay, even Pan checks his wild dance that he may not disturb the maiden's sleep. Having arrayed himself in fine purple and wreathed his head with roses, Dionysus comes to the side of Ariadne, drunk with love…"[98]

At the same time, the strong association of Bacchus (and it was almost exclusively in that Roman guise that the god was portrayed) "with feminine spirituality and power almost disappeared", as did "the idea that the destructive and creative powers of the god were indissolubly linked". Michelangelo's statue of Bacchus, dated 1496–97, typifies this trend. The god is a young and slightly effeminate man, his head wreathed with grapes. He holds up a wine cup and is- very obviously – drunk, having rolling eyes, open mouth and an unsteady gait – to the extent that he leans on a small supporting satyr. To some degree, though, this inebriated incapacity came later to be the characteristic of Silenus alone, allowing Bacchus to rise above the revels and remain rather more divine.[99]

98 Philostratus, *Imagines*, 1.15.1.
99 Bull, *The Mirror of the Gods*, 2006.

As the Reformation also coincided with the Renaissance, there was an influence of the former on the latter. Protestant churchmen attacked the Bacchic rites (and, indirectly, the humanism of the Italian Renaissance) for their idolatry, nakedness and licentiousness. Artists inevitably responded to this pressure: pictures of bacchanals often did not include maenads or they were relegated to a distinctly subsidiary role in Bacchus' train. Simultaneously, the bacchae's expression of female spirituality and power virtually vanished and the rites seemed to be reduced to groups of men sitting around drinking. Madness became merriment and Bacchus became synonymous with mere inebriation – scenes such as Silenus falling off his donkey, for instance.[100]

Titian's famous painting, *Bacchus and Ariadne* (1522–23), was early enough to escape this sort of moral censure. It is a curiously chaotic scene. The young god himself is portrayed as noble and athletic, leaping from his chariot with his eyes fixed on the girl. His retinue, however, tell a different story. A couple of maenads play cymbals and *tympana* to herald the god, but the rest of the *thiasos* seems to be completely out of control. Silenus slumps inebriated on his donkey; a servant struggles along behind him with a huge wine vase; an adult male satyr and a boy bring parts of a dismembered cow and a bearded, naked man wrestles with snakes.

In Titian's painting, then, everything other than the central lovers' encounter is slipping into the riot of the bacchanal – and it was, in fact, this aspect of the Bacchic story that proved the most attractive to painters over the ensuing centuries. Titian's *Bacchanal of the Andrians* (1523–26) is a relatively early example of this genre. The islanders have found that their spring now gives wine instead of water and as a result order is just beginning to break down. There is dancing and celebration, but in the foreground a small naked boy is being allowed to urinate into a

100 Bull, *The Mirror of the Gods*.

puddle of spilled wine next to a naked girl who has passed out, stretched full length on the ground with her head on an upturned vase. She has one hand behind her head, a pose that raises her bare breasts and imparts an abandoned and wanton air to her incapacity – clearly linking sex to over-indulgence in drink.

The downsides of too much alcohol often seem to be the main message that artists used Bacchus and his gang to convey. Jusepe de Ribera's *Drunken Silenus* (1626) is an obese older man, egged on by satyrs to have another glass; so too the reeling Silenus painted by Van Dyck. Rubens' *Bacchanalia* of 1616 adds in drunken satyrs as well: in the foreground two fleshy females sprawl, one of them unconscious whilst her infants try to breast feed.

These themes could bring a degree of secularisation with them as well. Diego Velázquez' *The Triumph of Bacchus* (*c.*1629) has the young god seated with some bibulous peasants, crowning one with ivy. He looks off uncomfortably to one side, as if feeling he's in the wrong company. Famously, Caravaggio dressed up one of his young lovers as the god, inviting the spectator to join him on the couch for a glass of wine. The same painter's self-portrait as a sick Bacchus takes this realism to a logical, if sordid, conclusion.

Another popular theme found from the early sixteenth century is the depiction of Bacchus and Ceres caring for love- often symbolised by Venus or Cupid. These images derive from a line in a comedy by the Roman playwright Terence;[101] it later became a popular proverb – especially after Luther used it. The epigram '*Sine Cerere et Baccho friget Venus*' ("without Ceres and Bacchus, Venus freezes") simply suggests that love needs food and wine to thrive. Artists widely took up the saying; one visual representation is by Hendrick Goltzius, dated 1600–1603; it's an intriguing painting as it seems to mimic a marble frieze and, moreover, one that is lit by torch light, although that torch is held by Cupid in the picture itself – a clever Mannerist conceit.

101 Publius Terentius Afer, *Eunuchus*, Act 4, scene 5.

Staying with this agrarian theme, and because of his association with the grape harvest, Bacchus lastly tended to become the god of autumn, and he and his followers often featured in sets of paintings depicting the seasons.

The iconographical parameters set by Renaissance art have rarely been expanded since. Bacchanals and bacchantes remained an ever-popular staple.[102] Bridging the gap into nineteenth century and after, which I will discuss separately, was Jean-Baptiste Greuze (1725–1805), who, true to his established style, cast his revellers as girls in their teens, typically with clothes and hair disarranged and one juvenile breast exposed, an expression of hesitant welcome on their faces. Greuze's broad contemporary, the sculptor Jean-Charles Marin (1759–1834), produced very similar images in terracotta and bronze. A host of bacchantes and bacchic nymphs, accompanied by bunches of grapes and frolicsome putti, bear his name. Most striking are a couple of busts of topless bacchantes, their young heads adorned with swags of grapes, their expressions ecstatic – mouths open and eyes partly shut. Whether they are drunk, in a trance or in the throes of sexual delight is unclear, but the figures underline the emerging sensuality of the genre.

Meanwhile, depictions of Bacchus, and of the god paired with Ariadne, continued into the seventeenth and eighteenth centuries, but thereafter tended to decline in popularity. English portrait painter Mary Beale (1633–99) portrayed a boy as the young deity in the 1660s; Charles Lucy (1692–1767) represented him as an effeminate youth and Simeon Solomon painted a very late head and shoulders of a girlish god in 1867.[103] Interest in scenes set on Naxos waned quite dramatically, so that when Pietro Benvenuti (1769–1844) selected the episode for a canvas in 1819, it was quite a daring and aberrant choice.

102 See, for example, bacchanalia painted by Ricci, Carpioni, Zuccarelli, Frangipane, Poussin (several times)

103 See too Sergei Solomko's *art nouveau* picture of a young, handsome Bacchus.

John Waterhouse painted Ariadne bored and alone on the island in 1898, but his interest was in a pretty red-haired girl baring a petite breast rather than in the passenger on the ship hoving into the harbour in the background. French artist Ker Xavier Roussel is notable for his very late depictions of a *Triumph of Bacchusm – fete champetre* (1911), *Drunken Silenus on a Donkey* (1925–27) and *Bacchanale* (1930).

NINETEENTH & TWENTIETH CENTURY IMAGES

During the late nineteenth and twentieth centuries, the aspects of the Dionysian story that repeatedly drew the attention of artists- even more than writers – were the drunkenness of bacchanals and the varied ecstatic states of the bacchantes – with emphasis upon their sexuality. The intoxicated and sensual undertones of these scenes have, especially, come to the fore. It has been claimed that when the maenads, banished from Renaissance art by religious disapproval, reappeared in nineteenth century art, they had been reduced to mere "simpering chorus girls." Is this fair, or correct?[104]

What could be painted was, for a long time, in large measure dictated by an oppressive public taste and morality. Some Victorian bacchanals are, accordingly, pretty tame – for example scenes by George Frederick Watts, William Etty or by William Salter. Watts and William Edward Frost in their time both presented something of a challenge to the art establishment with their nude studies, but their canvases remained chaste and elegant, nonetheless.[105]

---

104 Bull, *The Mirror of the Gods*, 2006.

105 Watts, *A Bacchanal; Nymphs & Satyrs Dancing; A Bacchante*; William Etty, *A Bacchante*; Salter, *A Bacchanal*, 1870; William Edward Frost, *Bacchanalian scene.*

Being a Bacchante

An early exception to the staid bacchante, however, is a portrait by George Romney (1734–1802) of Lady Emma Hamilton as a bacchante. Painted in 1785, she looks alluringly over her shoulder at the viewer, a winsome smile on her lips. Her thin blouse suggests a good deal of breast, but the sexual charge of the image is subtle. Hamilton was, in fact, quite notorious for dressing up as classical characters, especially as maenads. She posed as a bacchante with a tambourine for Élisabeth Vigée Le Brun in about 1790–92 and Romney also painted her as Circe and as Cassandra (with bared bosom).[106]

A very similar image to those of Hamilton is a portrait of the ballet dancer *Madame Bigottini as a Bacchante* by the prolific Jacques-Antoine Vallin (1760–1831). Vallin was a successor to Greuze, in that he seems to have churned out huge numbers of pictures of winsome young girls posed as bacchantes with one or both breasts exposed. He also produced quite a number of group scenes of maenads dancing with cupids or putti in classical and 'Arcadian' landscapes. Such scenes were, it seems, for Vallin merely an excuse to people them with naked girls. What comes over from all these portraits is the potential of classical scenes to evoke a bold and liberated sexuality, although it took some while for this fully to be expressed in art.

At the same time, though, blatant sexuality didn't have to be conveyed. Posing as a participant in a bacchanal was clearly fashionable at all levels of society in the late eighteenth century-as witnessed by William Hoare's *Lady Emily Kerr as a Bacchante,* 1770, the Swiss painter Angelica Kauffman's self-portrait as a bacchante, the portrait of *Madame Cail as a Bacchante* by Louis-Marie Sicardi (1746–1825), the German engraver Georg David Matthieu's *Anna Regina von Olthoff as a Bacchante* (c.1760)

106 See too Vigée Le Brun's 1785 *Bacchante* at the Clark Art Institute in Williamstown.

or Jean Raoux' portrait of the dancer *Mademoiselle Prevost as a Bacchante* (1723). The fashion didn't die out completely for quite a while, either – witness Julia Margaret Cameron's early photographic study of a 'bacchante' and the portrait of Edwardian soldier's wife, *Mrs Ralph Peto as a Bacchante,* painted in 1910 by John Lavery.

Why did these women wish to be commemorated as bacchae? It seems likely that the bacchante was exotic and was associated with concepts of being daring and independent. The sexual frisson added to this, undoubtedly, but it was not the main connotation in the eighteenth century, at least. For the dancers portrayed, a certain degree of undress and physical allure was likely to have been stock in trade. However, Lady Kerr seems to have come from Scottish aristocracy and the von Olthoff family were prominent government officials in the Swedish Pomeranian town of Stralsund. They clearly had reputations to preserve, so that anything too immoral is unlikely- especially for Lady Kerr, young teenage daughter of the Marquess of Lothian. The fun of dressing up may well have been an element: Anna Regina's brother, Adolf Friedrich, was portrayed as a Turk around the same period. The pictures may also have suggested that the sitter was a cultured and educated character, acquainted with classical myths and ancient civilisations.

Neo-Classicists

From the mid-nineteenth century, with the rise of the neo-classicist painters, British art saw a sudden expansion in depictions of Greek and Roman nudity and of increasingly frenzied maenads. Sir Lawrence Alma-Tadema was particularly prolific in this respect, and it has been noted that his bacchic women represent "the most sensuous of his works." This makes them just as attractive to modern audiences as they were to many Victorians, who appreciated their tasteful eroticism. Not all of

Alma-Tadema's contemporaries approved, though. John Ruskin felt that they emulated all that was insipid and immoral about classical culture. The pictures showed "the last corruption of the Roman state, and its bacchanalian phrenzy, which Mr Alma-Tadema seems to hold it his heavenly mission to portray." [107]

Alma-Tadema painted several bacchantes, two of which are especially notable. His 1873 canvas, *Exhausted Maenides,* shows three women fast asleep after a bacchanalia. One is completely naked; the other two are partially unclothed. Their exhaustion and oblivion are obvious. The same painter's *Bacchante* of 1907 is a close-up of a breathless looking red-head (modelled by his wife) who regards us from the corners of her eyes in a slightly distracted but intriguing manner. She has a leopard fur robe and cymbals and might very well be supposed to be succumbing to the trance-like state induced by the music and dancing. Alma-Tadema's *Bacchante Dancing Before the Thymele* (which was an altar in a theatre) depicts a girl wrapped in leopard skins and waving torches, an oddly fetishised sort of pose that the painter often used. Lord Leighton painted a broadly similar bacchante, who is pictured playing with a fawn, a setting which has the decided effect of toning down any thoughts of frenzy that the title might initially prompt. Another *Bacchante,* painted in 1888 by John Reinhard Weguelin (1849–1927), is a further example of the more restrained type of maenad. She wears a leopard skin over her dress and has an ivy wreath on her brow, but she seems otherwise unfrenzied and sober, unless her pose gripping the base of a column indicates faintness after the rites.

Even more interesting than these single figures may be Alma-Tadema's recreations of the Dionysian rites. His *Bacchant at a Harvest Festival* is a perfectly restrained and decorous picture, despite the image of a fur-draped woman waving a tambourine

107 Vern G Swanson, *Sir Lawrence Alma-Tadema*, 1977, 50; J.G. Lovett & W.R. Johnston, *Empires Restored, Elysium Revisited – The Art of Sir Lawrence Alma-Tadema*, 1991, 73; Ruskin, *Works*, 1908, vol.33, 322.

over her wreathed head; in contrast, the *Dedication to Bacchus* of 1889 begins to suggest something wilder. The artist presents several fur-robed maenads orchestrating the presentation of large votive wineskin to the god. *Tympana* and torches are waved aloft; two women dance to the sound of music that is provided by a throng of young maenads with double flutes and percussion. The main officiating priestess brandishes a fennel stem adorned with ribbons. The marble, candelabras and heaped up pomegranates are all suggestive of the temple's wealth and opulence. A little nude girl with golden Pre-Raphaelite hair in the audience is having the ceremony explained to her by her mother. Her naked presence, albeit slightly veiled with a purple scarf, reminds us that classical Greece was far off in time, space and manners. Not only is the public nudity alien to us, but *The Times* in its review of the picture at the Royal Academy described how "a little child [is] about to be handed over to the priestess and her attendants, who are grouped around the altar of Dionysus." This might raise the horrible possibility that the intention is to sacrifice her, but the picture is sometimes subtitled *Initiation of a Priestess,* so that it happily appears that the girl is about to be initiated into the ministry of the cult. Her nakedness, therefore, may be interpreted as a quitting of her former life and a presentation of herself, pure and fresh, to the god- hence the celebrations of her friends and family who accompany her.[108]

We may compare the *Dedication to Bacchus* to Sir William Blake Richmond's scene, *Procession in Honour of Bacchus at the Time of Vintage* (1869), which tackles a very similar public event at a temple. It is rather more static than Alma-Tadema's, with the figures lined up across the picture almost in silhouette, but the presence of several nude children again underlines the exotic and alien nature of the rites. Interestingly, in 1871 Alma-Tadema painted a canvas of similar dimensions and title to Richmond's –

108 *The Times*, May 25th, 1889, 10; E. Swinglehurst, *Lawrence Alma-Tadema*, 2001, 79.

The Vintage Festival (the first in a series of which the *Dedication* is a later part). Large vases of wine are being paraded into a temple in Pompeii to the music of pipes and tambourines. It is a very respectable and orderly scene, this time, the only hints of frenzy being a thyrsos that has been cast down rather carelessly in the corner right foreground – and the crowd assembled beyond the doorway on the far right of the picture, who await the start of the orgy.[109] The artist followed this with *Autumn Vintage Festival* in 1877. The picture a close-up study of a bacchante holding a torch dancing before an altar with a jug of wine. Thirdly, we may note Alma-Tadema's diploma piece for the Royal Academy – *The Way to the Temple* – which he submitted on April 19th 1882. The main figure is a votive statue seller sitting quietly on her own, vine leaves circling her splendid red hair, but in the background a procession of male and female bacchantes passes, noisily, one with a thyrsos, two with *tympana*. Subsequently, in 1900, Richmond began a picture comparable with Alma-Tadema's *Exhausted Maenides,* mentioned earlier. The unfinished *Dionysus and Maenads* shows the god standing in a grove, amidst naked women sprawled all around, asleep wherever they collapsed. It effectively captures the profound fatigue the rites would have caused.

Paintings of Greek festival processions were a popular theme at this time: in 1875 Lord Leighton exhibited the *Daphnephoria,* a painting of an Athenian ceremony held in honour of Apollo. Although all these linear designs bear considerable resemblance to Greek friezes, it was probably Leighton who had initiated the fashion when, in 1855, he painted *Cimabue's Celebrated Madonna Carried in Procession* – an early Renaissance incident. The impact of this painting is attested by the fact that when Sir William Blake Richmond, who was already heavily influenced by Leighton, decided to paint the *Procession in Honour of Bacchus,* he hired the

109 E. Prettejohn & P. Trippi, *Lawrence Alma-Tadema – At Home in Antiquity*, 2016; Swinglehurst, *Lawrence Alma-Tadema*, 70–71.

same studio that his mentor had used when working on *Cimabue.* In 1894 Alma-Tadema painted *Spring,* which depicts a procession to the temple of Flora during the Roman festival of Cerealia. The group carry two satyr herms, who each have a winnowing basket full of fruit and bear the infant Dionysos on their shoulders. The procession is fronted by a large group of little girls, each also bearing a *liknon* from which they scatter flowers. The simple joy of this event, with its high proportion of infant celebrants, contrasts quite strongly with most others honouring the god.

Also in 1871, Alma-Tadema painted another *Bacchanal*, this time depicting a private rather than a public rite. We see people dancing in a courtyard to the sound (of course) of pipes and a tambourine. One of the celebrants has already succumbed to the drink, lying prone on the ground with a wine jug still gripped in his hands, but it honestly doesn't seem likely that the other 'bacchae' will be joining him on the ground – the lead couple are male and female who look for all the world like a Victorian husband and wife who've dressed up in Greek costume for charades. Perhaps unconsciously, another figure underlines the well-established association that exists between bacchantes and excess. In the background of *The Roses of Heliogabalus,* just as the mad emperor releases the cascade of petals that are to smother his guests, there is a pipe playing woman dressed in maenad fashion in leopard skin. The banquet depicted has nothing to do with the bacchic rites, so the picture simply betrays how these women have come to be regarded: wherever there is a hint of depravity, there you'll find the bacchae.

Over and above the representations of the maenads at their most frenzied, there are pictures that show them as calmer and more measured ministers to the god. Alma-Tadema's *Calling the Worshippers* of 1892 is one such image. A woman clad in a leopard skin, with an ivy chaplet on her brow, stands at the foot of some marble steps, having apparently just issued a blast on what looks like a bugle. At the top of the staircase, two more animated priestesses stand talking, awaiting the arrival of the congregation. However, this painting alerts us to the possibility that Alma-Tadema used the furs and wreaths simply as a sign that a woman was a priestess of one of the Greek deities. This seems definitely to be the case in *On the Road to the Temple of Ceres* (1879), in which- were it not for the title – the presence of animal skins and tympana might mislead us. In the 1912 canvas, *Preparation in the Colosseum,* a stern looking 'bacchante' in fur and ivy wreath stands thoughtfully besides a huge brazier and piles of fruit; she might in fact be a more generic 'priestess,' having nothing to do with the bacchic rites.

Perhaps the most significant of all Alma-Tadema's Bacchic scenes is the *Women of Amphissa* of 1887, which takes its inspiration from the story of Plutarch described in Part One (by way of George Eliot's *Daniel Deronda* chapter 17) and which Ursula Le Guin examined in verse. The maenads are just beginning to awaken, having slept wherever they had collapsed at the end of their frenzied dancing. This is very much the morning after the night before: the bacchae look blearily at the town's women who have been guarding them overnight and who now offer food and drink. The picture nicely encapsulates the hangover that was always likely to have followed the ecstasies of the rite. There is, in point of fact, little direct evidence of the worship of Dionysos in the picture. There are ivy-wreaths, leopard skins, a tympanum and, very subtly, two thyrsoi which form the poles supporting the canopy of a market stall.

The last canvas by Alma-Tadema that we'll consider is an interesting contrast in tone to all that has preceded. *Between Venus and Bacchus* (1882) shows us a moment of peace during the bacchic festivities. A couple have found themselves alone in a courtyard by a large ornamental fountain. The young man of the pair holds aloft a thyrsos, but looks intently at his partner, a bacchante with tympanum and ivy wreath, who has paused to gaze reflectively into the water of the basin surrounding a statue of the goddess (modelled upon the famous Venus of Rhodes). Love is in the air, it seems, distracting the two from their devotions to Dionysos.

John William Godward, a further late Victorian classicist, painted numerous female figures that were identified as bacchantes or who suggested Dionysian connections. Godward specialised in curvy, sexy women who were naked or whose ample nudity was only partially veiled by see-through fabrics. *At the Gate of the Temple* (1898) shows a fully clothed woman holding a thyrsos; his *Priestess of Bacchus* (1890) is also decently dressed, but she is plainly recovering from the frenzied dancing of the rite, as she reclines limply on a marble bench, barely able to support her thyrsos. Many of Godward's more revealing figures hold tambourines, evocative of the bacchic revels – for example, *Ionian Dancer* (1902), *Drusilla* and *Tambourine Girl* (1906). *A Priestess* (1893) calmly confronts us face-on, topless and proud as she holds her tall thyrsos. A highly comparable image is *Young Bacchante with Thyrsus* painted in 1899 by the German Max Nonnenbruch (1857–1922). She too is bare-chested and with an imperious expression on her face. The string of pearls around her neck somewhat undermines the pseudo-classical air, however.

Godward's nudes had an understated sexuality, but this was not guaranteed by the mere fact of nudity. We might here contrast the work of the painter Henrietta Rae; she painted naked females who largely lacked any sensuality or sensuousness at all. Her *Bacchante* of 1885, for example, may be holding a thyrsos whilst picking grapes to make wine for the excesses of the Dionysian rites, but she looks like a Victorian lady in her conservatory who just happens to have forgotten to get dressed. The same might be said of the Spaniard Joaquin Sorolla's *Bacchante* of 1886; it is a fine academic nude, but the woman seems isolated and static.[110] A pleasant contrast to these is the *Bacchante* painted by Edith

110 Likewise, the *Bacchante* by Thomas Kennington (1856–1915) or by Mary Cassatt (1872).

Ridley Corbet (1846–1920), an artist whose work showed the influence of Alma-Tadema. Corbet painted classical females in see-through garments and her bacchante is in fact, topless, seated in a glade as she dresses her thyrsos with ivy. It's an attractive picture: a moment of calm before the frenzy.

Bacchae Abroad

Bacchantes abounded across the breadth of European art during this period. The French academic painter Guillaume Bouguereau painted at least half a dozen such figures, although they are generally quite demure and respectable, the exception being a naked example who is resting on the ground, playing with a lively goat that rears above her – an image that seems to imply a wild- if not transgressive – sensuality, but in the most subtle of terms. Bouguereau also tackled a *Youth of Bacchus,* which comprises a flurry of dancing and excited nudes. Silenus slumps from his donkey on one side and at the other centaurs play pipes for the gyrating nymphs.

A figure comparable figure to Bouguereau's caprine maenad is a *Bacchanal* by the Swede Julius Kronberg (1850–1921), featuring a topless maenad who is embracing a goat seated beside her. The same artist's *Temple Dancer* from 1890 shows us another bacchante, dressed in standard animal skin and ivy leaf chaplet. She is slumped against the wall of the temple, her thyrsos held loosely across her lap, very clearly worn out by her exertions – although her sideways gaze suggests that the dancing is continuing nearby. Italian classicist Giovanni Muzzioli painted an amusing study of the *Temple of Bacchus* in 1881. Rather as in Kronberg's temple, the rites seem well advanced, with the precinct littered with fallen ivy leaves, lost items of clothing, discarded wine jugs, drinking cups and even a thyrsos. In the foreground a man has passed out, crumpled against the pedestal of a huge urn. A slightly manic maenad is dancing in front of him, brandishing her thyrsos and tympanum, but he is utterly oblivious to her presence. Behind them, another man is unconscious at the base of an altar, whilst the dancing still swirls frenetically in the background. In 1886 the same artist painted a *Bacchanalia,* another scene set in a temple but this time featuring a male celebrant slightly less inebriated than those seen before. All the same, he appears to be unable to stand up and catches slightly optimistically at the hem of a bacchante's dress as she dances past. She laughs down at him, but appears unlikely to stop. In these two paintings, Muzzioli surely gives us some sense of what the later stages of the orgies must have looked and felt like.

The world of mythology and fantasy has always provided a pretext for artists to paint nudes and to indulge their imaginations. If those activities could be combined, so much the better. French painter Jean-Léon Gérôme took advantage of this with his *Bacchante* of 1853; it is a slightly disturbing depiction of a young woman who has curling ram's horns emerging from her wavy hair. Ettore Forti (1850–1940) displayed his familiarity with the Dionysian myths when he chose to paint a cheery maenad riding on the back of a centaur. She looks to be playfully goading him along with her thyrsos as they hurry towards a revel. The sexual attraction of human women to mythical creatures implied here was nothing new. Such images had been selected from the classical myths as far back as the Renaissance-as works by Annibale Carracci and Nicolas Poussin demonstrate. During the nineteenth century they were also exploited by the Portuguese Victor Meirelles, whose naked *Bacchante* of 1858 is being awoken from her slumber by a faun with a bunch of grapes; by the German artist Johann Wilhelm Tischbein (1751–1829) who painted maenads and fauns cavorting together; by Bouguereau, who depicted a *Faun and Bacchante* embracing (1860) and by Hungarian Gyula Benczur who showed a drunken, nude bacchante being ogled lasciviously by satyrs (1881).

Benczur's compatriot, Mihaly Zichy (1827–1906) created the most memorable of these scenes: his *Bacchante* laughs wildly as a satyr grabs her and sucks her breast.

In truth, though, it remained the case that the label 'Bacchante' or 'Maenad' often just provided an excuse for painting a naked woman, as in Polish painter Henryk Piatkowski's *Maenad* of 1876. The same might be said of Sorolla's *Bacchante en Reposo,* which is nothing more than a naked woman on a bed, and Ferdinand Leeke's *Bacchante* – a woman draped in leopard skin and stretching as if after a deep sleep – but really, it's just an excuse for a nude study. Whether we should view the *Bacchante* by French academic classicist Camille Felix Bellanger (1853–1923) is a nice point. She's a well-formed woman sitting with her tambourine, arms raised to emphasise her bosom. She grins invitingly at the viewer, but so does the head of the herm by which she's sitting, leaving us a little uncertain as to whether we're viewing reality or fantasy. Perhaps we catch her at the point that her ecstasy unites her with the deity.

Violent Femmes

Another British classicist painter, a contemporary of Leighton and Alma-Tadema, was Edward Poynter. He had his initial training in Paris, under the Swiss-born artist Charles Gleyre (1806–1874). Specialising in orientalist, biblical and mythological scenes, Gleyre was a very slow and considered painter and ceased to exhibit works publicly after 1849, in order to concentrate on teaching in his studio. His last displayed work was *La Danse des bacchantes* of that year, a picture that epitomises the modern view of this Dionysian rites. It is set in the mountains and features only female maenads, who are dancing at the foot of a tall column bearing a figure of the older, bearded Dionysos.[111]

111 Contrast some dancing maenads by Cornelis Lens (1739–1822) who circle a male figure- albeit it one who seems to be transforming into a laurel tree.

The women wear furs and wreaths around their heads; some are naked, others may be in the process of losing their clothes. The ritual would appear to be reaching its climax: a couple of the dancers have already collapsed with exhaustion and the central figure, a completely nude woman, is pictured leaping into the air, her head thrown back in ecstasy, a thyrsos in one hand. All the celebrants are shown deeply absorbed in the ceremony. Gleyre's scene is rather unusual, as is his 1864 canvas – *Pentheus Pursued by Maenads.* Painters were happy to presents the bacchae as wild, naked women, exploiting their latent eroticism, but they generally shied away from the more violent aspects of their mythology. Not so in this case: the king flees in obvious panic, six women in close pursuit and calling out to more. One grips a dagger as well as a thyrsos, making it clear what the man's fate will soon be. It is chilling – and rare. Gleyre did paint a much more conventional *Bacchante* (*c.*1860) as well; she's a curvy red-head playing her pipes alone in a wood, an attractive but unremarkable work.

The maenads in murderous mode were a subject which seems once to have been popular but which gradually fell from public taste, perhaps because it jarred with the increasingly prevalent perception of the bacchantes as carnally aroused rather than inflamed with blood-lust. Readers may recall that Orpheus was murdered by bassarids because of an act of perceived blasphemy and this scene was handled by several painters including Parmigianino (1503–40), Massimo Stanzione (1585–1656) Valerio Castello (1624–59), Gregorio Lazzarini (1667–1730), Josef Bergler (1753–1829) and Luigi Ademollo (1764–1849), who depicted the demise of Pentheus. When French academic classicists Emile Levy and Emil-Jean Baptiste Philippe Bin tackled the death of Orpheus in 1866 and 1874 respectively, the pictures were extremely late specimens of the theme. Both display a strong sado-masochist air, the naked, exulting women extravagantly beating the fallen, helpless man. The most recent example of this subject that I have found is Felix Vallotton's gruesome *Orpheus*

Dismembered, painted in 1914. The young man is pinned down by the women's thyrsoi; blood flows as two of the maenads claw at his back with their nails and others have collected rocks with which to stone him to death

Sleeping Beauties

Bacchantes became more physical and passionate as the century neared its end, but this wasn't an entirely new phenomenon. Certain artists, whose style already accommodated the erotic, had long ago identified the potentiality of such scenes. A good example is French court painter Francois Boucher, whose *Bacchante Playing a Reed Pipe* is typical of his pink and voluptuously nude reclining girls. Boucher's contemporary, Jean-Simon Berthelemy (1743–1811) depicted a naked *Reclining Bacchante Playing the Cymbals* which is very similar; his *Bacchante* picking grapes is semi-clothed and meets the viewer's regard with a saucy look.

Now, for centuries artists have painted women lying on beds, regarding the observer with an enticing expression – famous examples include Titian's *Venus of Urbino, Venus with the Organ Player* and *Danae* and, much later, Manet's *Olympia.* A development of this genre was the sleeping female, as exemplified by pictures of the *Sleeping Venus* by Titian and Giorgione. In these canvases, the woman remains naked, but her recumbent and unconscious state adds extra notes of voyeurism and, I suspect, a suggestion of vulnerability to sexual assault. This was something which appeared quite regularly in nineteenth century art.

A fore-runner may be the aptly titled *Wanton Bacchante* by Sir Joshua Reynolds, a picture which has claims to epitomise the entire bacchante style. A pretty nude is curled up languidly on a bed set in the open air. Cupid is speaking to her and she regards him with a quizzical expression, her nakedness only made more apparent by a bracelet around her upper arm. An unashamedly sexual view of the maenads is also displayed by Edward Calvert in his *Bacchante with Lyre* of 1829. Calvert was an artist who appreciated a nice bottom – as his *Primitive City* (1822) and *Bride* (1828) attest. The bacchante looks over her shoulder at us, as if inviting us to follow her into wood ahead.

In 1864, Pierre-Honore Hugrel (1827–1921) depicted a highly sensual *Bacchante* reclined on a bank, her arms thrown back above her head, where she holds her thyrsos, her gaze very much engaging that of the viewer. In a second canvas on the subject, in 1887 Joaquin Sorolla depicted a *Bacchante* stretched out, relaxing by herself on fabrics on a marble terrace, her tambourine held above her head as she amuses herself. The Pole Witold Priszkowski painted a gorgeous and sensuous *Bacchante* in 1855, a voluptuous nude luxuriating on a bed of rich fabrics the light playing on her through a veil. In 1865 Jean-Baptiste Corot painted two versions of a *Bacchante in a Landscape*, in which some sort of bacchanal is taking place far in the background behind in the reclining figure, and a very similar *Bacchante by the Sea*, a nude lying alone on leopard skins, watching waves lap the shore. He also painted *Bacchante with a Panther* in 1860, a curious tableau in which the naked woman reclines on the ground, holding up a dead bird to tempt the large cat – which is being ridden by a small child (using reins). French-Polish artist Paul Merwart in 1887 painted *Bacchante with Grapes*, another well-built nude lying on the seashore on leopard skins, but this time contemplating a bunch of fruit that she holds in the air above her.

From the eighteenth century onwards, the fashion arose for even more suggestive scenes depicting bacchic females at rest. Fragonard, for example, painted a *Sleeping Bacchante* in the late eighteenth century: she is a single, almost naked, figure slumped against some piled up fabric. Her inviting air of sexual vulnerability is the very evident subtext of the image. Jean Jacques Lagrenee (1739–1831) painted a very similar figure. Rene Gaillard (1719–90) engraved a scene of *Les bacchantes endormies,* which adapted a common scenario of satyrs spying on sleeping nymphs by replacing them with four naked and intertwined maenads. The tone of voyeurism and veiled sexual threat are tangible.

Eugen Felix's *Sleeping Bacchante*, dated 1868, is a fine study of a splendid nude; her body is twisted erotically and her arms are extended behind her head. This latter posture has a double effect: it lifts and emphasises her bust, but it also makes her seem more approachable- it might be read as inviting rather than defensive. Two Hungarian painters took the theme of the unconscious maenad even further. Karoly Lotz (1833–1904), painted a highly erotic *Sleeping Bacchante,* her arms thrown out behind her head, her body twisted towards us with her thighs parted; from Karoly Brocky (1808–55) we have a sensual *Sleeping Bacchante* (1850–55). She is a young female, shown only from her chest upwards. Her head falls backwards, her arms thrown out, her breasts raised and mouth slightly open. She may be awakening, but it is easy to suppose she is overwhelmed by ecstasy, the cause of which lies outside the frame.

Drink can be a major factor in the helpless slumber of many of these bacchantes – the rites of Bacchus will inevitably involve a good deal of wine. The Austrian painter Eugen Felix (1836–1906) depicted the run-up to this: his *Two Bacchantes* are naked, offering a herm of Pan wine from a beaker and grapes, whilst a goat bucks pointedly in the background. French orientalist and classicist Emile Meyer painted a very similar scene in 1892. Arthur Hacker's *Bacchante* of 1913 is still standing, just- she's supported by her thyrsos, but her chin has slumped onto her chest and she holds an empty wine bowl at angle which would spill the drink – if there was any left.

The inebriation that followed from such libations had far greater interest for many artists though. Thomas Rowlandson's *Bacchante* of 1787 verges on the pornographic, the drunken woman is slumped against a tree with her bare groin thrust towards the viewer. Hans Makart's *Resting Bacchante* of 1863 lies on furs, her tambourine cast aside and a wine cup held out for a refill. Cesare Maccare (1840–1919) presents us with a *Bacchante* (1870) who, whilst being fully clothed, lies back on cushions, a wine cup held loosely on her lap, her lips parted and her eyes partly closed. In 1882 the French artist Adolphe Alexandre Lesrel (1839–1929) created *The Drunken Bacchante,* a richly coloured and highly erotic scene in which the naked woman reclines amidst flowers and grapes, her empty goblet held above her.

In 1847 Gustave Courbet used his sister as model when he drew the *Head of a Sleeping Bacchante* in chalk. She has fallen asleep sitting upright, fully clothed, and is only really identifiable as a maenad by the vine leaves around her head. This very respectable image contrasts strongly with his oil painting *La Bacchante* – a full length and voluptuous nude who lies prostrate and insensible on the ground, some grapes and an empty wine cup lying near her right hand.

Frenzied Dancing

How the maenads got so worked up was always a source of lascivious fascination top artists and their customers. Antoine-Francois Callet (1741–1823) painted a *Bacchante with Cymbals* in 1778. She seems to have reached the peak of the Dionysian frenzy. Her thyrsos and a wine flagon have been cast aside, she leans against an altar to Pan, arching backwards towards it and flaunting her naked body in a delightfully abandoned manner.

Other artists of the same period were drawn to the same loss of self-consciousness that the rites provoked. A Rococo bas relief by Clodion, entitled *Bacchanalian Games,* has women and satyrs leaping wildly through hoops. The German Johann William Tischbein painted an unusually acrobatic *Maenad Dance* around the same time. The semi-naked women are tumbling and performing handstands to the sound of their companions' drums. Tischbein also painted a lively dance of bacchantes and satyrs, but it lacks the gymnastic novelty of this previous work.

The German Ferdinand Leeke (1859–1923) twice handled scenes of bacchic frenzy. The canvas titled *Three Nymphs in a Glade* shows a trio of wild-eyed maenads, dashing and dancing in a deranged manner. A painting known as *Spring Dance* is very similar – although there are more fur-clad, thyrsos wielding maenads and they look slightly less frantic. In *La fete des bois – les bacchantes,* a large canvas by British artist, Frederick Bridgman (1847–1928), a host of ecstatic maenads cavort through a wood. They are accompanied by three lions – a topless woman rides the male, using a length of ivy stem as a rein; a lioness pads along behind, watching rather warily as another frenzied woman waves a cub in the air, holding it by the scruff of its neck. The whole scene teeters on the verge of comedy – or disaster.

Like Bridgman's scene, John Collier's *Maenads* of 1886 truly seems to capture some sense of their frenzy and unbound nature. A group of fifteen or more are careering through a forest, partially draped in animal skins – although largely bare-breasted. They have wreaths in their wild hair, two leopards on leashes and one woman brandishes aloft her arms, around which are coiled snakes. Their progress looks precipitate and directionless: in the background, one of this group has stumbled and at least one of the big cats seems to have decided that it's had enough and has laid down. Many of the maenads are waving thyrsoi; one of them has even thrown hers for a tame goat to fetch, rather like a dog. It's a slightly bizarre and helter-skelter scene.

The American artist Robert Frederick Blum painted a *Vintage Festival Bacchanalia* in about 1888, a bright, colourful composition notable for the fact that it shows a mixed group of celebrants. A procession of women bearing thyrsoi and playing instruments is preceded by two men who leap exuberantly in the air; two little naked girls accompany them – one plays the cymbals and the other carries a small goat (presumably a sacrifice). Sheffield painter and illustrator Fred Hammersley Ball engraved a pleasant *Bacchante* pirouetting with two *tympana* in

1914. A strong breeze seems to be bending the trees behind her and tugging at her dress and hair, so that the whole scene is a whirl of energetic movement.

The ultimate consequence of all this drink and dance may be seen in Cesare Ciani's *Classical Interior – Bacchante Holding a Thyrsos*. The bacchante in question is slumped on a bed or couch, looking despondent, limp and listless. What's particularly notable about the picture is that the figure appears to be a boy – or otherwise a prepubescent girl. American artist Robert van Vorst Sewell (1860–1924), tackled a similar scene in *Exhausted Bacchantes* of 1924. Two slightly bewildered looking nudes are just stirring from sleep in a woodland glade. Emile Laporte (1841–1919) in *Le reveil de la bacchante* ('The awakening bacchante') also portrayed a very curvy young maenad's recovery. In this case, though, she doesn't look the worse for wear at all- she smiles in a very welcoming way at the viewer, suggesting that more ecstasy is entirely possible.

Marble Maenads

Perhaps because of the possibilities offered by three dimensional representations, sculptures of bacchantes have sometimes been amongst the most erotic and provocative. Jean-Baptiste Clesinger's *Recumbent Bacchante* of 1848 could easily be a soft porn centrefold. The work is subtitled *Woman Stung by a Snake,* and there is indeed a snake curled around her wrist, but as she writhes on a bed of grapes and vine leaves, her large breasts heaving and her lips parted, she looks far more like an inebriated woman in the throes of orgasm. Novelist Théophile Gautier, who was acquainted with the model, the well-known Madame Sabatier, praised the work lavishly as one of the most beautiful pieces of modern sculpture: "it is a pure orgiastic frenzy, the wild-haired maenad is winding herself around the feet of Bacchus, the father of freedom and joy… A powerful spasm of happiness causes the young woman's ample bosom to swell, giving prominence to gleaming breasts..."

The *Recumbent Bacchante* by Lorenzo Bartolini, of about 1834, is much less erotic but no less sensual. She is an elegant young woman, stretched out on a bed with a tambourine and (perhaps obligatory) snake. Passionate embraces between pairs of bacchantes and satyrs or fauns were also popular – see, by way of illustration, examples by Georges Jacquot or by James Pradier (1833). Such sculptures don't always have to be pneumatic and orgasmic, of course: Joseph Antoine Bernard in 1919 carved a charming *Bacchante* holding a bunch of grapes who is pubescent girl with little breasts, plump tummy and awkward podgy legs.

Nonetheless, French sculptor Auguste Rodin went a stage further and, perhaps, reached a logical conclusion – considering many of the perceptions of maenads we have discussed. His *Bacchantes Embracing* (*Bacchantes s'enlaçant*) of about 1896 shows a naked maenad in the arms of her lover – who is, in fact, a female faun. A copy of this sculpture is owned by the Brooklyn Museum, which also has on display another work by Rodin, *Damned Women*. This is a second lesbian pair, caught in the moment of collapsing onto bed together, and is named after the poem by Baudelaire that was mentioned earlier.

Interestingly, Spanish ceramics company Lladro still offer sensual figures of dreamy bacchantes riding leopard sand panthers, a fact which underlines the continued demand for such feminine and sensual figures.

Modern Maenads

Various artistic trends emerged in the twentieth century. One, in Britain, was an austerely cool classical style for representing the Greek gods. Examples include Joseph Southall's *Bacchus and Ariadne* (1912), Harry Morley's *Young Bacchus* (1930) and *Bacchanal* (1932) and Charles Shannon's *Childhood of Bacchus*

(1919). Shannon's close companion, Charles Ricketts, produced the most interesting picture of this group. His *Bacchus in India* (1913), shows the god reclining on an elephant whilst all around him the overwhelmed maenads swirl. This Bacchus is young, but he is lean and severe, rising above the drunken riot and clearly a conqueror.

A less severe and chilly aesthetic was found amongst the German Expressionists. Lovis Corinth (1858–1925) painted and drew a number of bacchanals, all of which featured naked figures in varying degrees of intoxication and debauch. His nudes are refreshingly real – they are not ideal nymphs but rather paunchy males and solid, slightly coarsened women with sagging breasts. His *Bacchantenpaar* of 1908 comprises a plainly middle couple, very jolly after a good drink. Even Corinth's rendering of *Ariadne auf Naxos* (1913) has the heroine slumped naked, her legs apart, looking more like she has been overcome by wine than *ennui* (contrast Waterhouse's canvas on the same theme mentioned earlier).

German symbolist Franz von Stuck drew figures very similar to those of Corinth- young, old, pretty and ugly, as seen in his etching *Bacchantes, Satyrs and Nymphs,* a reeling and staggering procession of dancers. His *Bacchanal* of 1905 depicts a circle of dancers in front of a classical portico; one of the naked frenzied females is just at the point of collapsing into the arms of a companion.

Polish symbolist Wilhelm Kotarbinski (1848–1921) also preferred a vision of history that was more concerned with excess and extremes – see for instance his canvases *A Roman Orgy, An Orgy in the Time of the Caesars* (1872) and *An Orgy on the Island of Capri in the Time of Tiberius* (1882), the last of which features murdered victims as well as the usual frenzied maenadic dancing. These canvases look for all the world like scenes from the Hollywood spectaculars that were to succeed them in the next century. Fellow Pole, Henryk Siemradski (1843–1902), by contrast painted a bright and jubilant *Bacchanal* in 1890, in which all his characters disport in a sunny, pastoral landscape with carefree and convivial joy.

Corinth appears, in some sense, to have created the milieu in which any form of sexuality and any degree of nudity might be presented. Swedish painter Gerda Roosval-Kallstenius imagined a *Bacchanal* at sunset, with maenads and satyrs cavorting together. Paul Cezanne's *Bacchanal* of 1875–80 is also called 'The Battle of Love' and this subtitle more accurately reflects the scene he painted- what we may in fact be witnessing is a mass rape of nymphs by satyrs. At best, the couples are extremely lively and vigorous in their lovemaking, in which passion verges on wrestling. Belgian artist Auguste Leveque (1866–1921) painted two canvases titled *Bacchanalia*, which are both a mass of writhing flesh and sensual delight. Races and ages are mixed promiscuously in a tangle of entwined bodies. Leveque's *Sleeping Bacchantes* shows the aftermath – four naked women collapsed on the ground outdoors. Ivor Henry Thomas Hele (1912–1993) created a very similar *Bacchanalia* in which the frenzy seems to have spread from the maenads and satyrs to the animals with them. The scene suggests a cacophony of noise – cries, cymbals and bellowing beasts – all at the point of imminent collapse. Slightly more restrained is the 1918 *Bacchanal* of Stephen Haweis (1877–1969), a watercolour that subtly evokes the swirling movement of its tattooed participants – even so, one man grabs his partner's breasts and another is steadied by his companion as he gyrates. French Cubist Andre Lhote in 1912 painted his own modernist interpretation of a *Bacchante.* She's a well-rounded woman seen lying in a landscape, surrounded by playing cards, grapes and other fruit. For all its radical style, it preserves many traditional features of such a subject.

Pablo Picasso was drawn to bacchic scenes repeatedly after 1945, when he was living in the south of France. He once remarked, "It is strange, in Paris I never draw fauns, centaurs, or mythical heroes... [but] they always seem to live in these parts."[112] His *Bacchanal with Acrobat* (1959) features a pipe player and two tumblers, plus an enigmatic goat in the background. Another version bearing the same date adds a black bull, making clear Picasso's familiarity with the detailed mythology and symbolism of Dionysos. In a third variant that's in the National Gallery of Scotland, the goat has joined the dancing; other versions feature coupling lovers, owls and a mother and child. The artist was very clearly fascinated, if not obsessed, with this theme.

Picasso's strong attraction to the bacchic rites is confirmed by two related lithograph *Bacchanals,* both dated 1956, which depict a male and female bacchante pair entwined in ecstasy to the sound of a satyr's flute. *La Bacchanale* of 1957 depicts a true orgy, with at least a dozen figures and a number of goats; the wine is flowing, fruit is being passed around and a tambourine is being struck. On the right of the picture some darker skinned figures – very possibly satyrs – appear to be in the process of seizing and overwhelming the rest of the celebrants. Issued in 1956, but drawn in 1933, is another lithograph depicting a mature male (perhaps a god) reclining against a younger woman, whilst a man and a woman dance before them with a bull. All the participants in this bacchanal are, of course, naked. Lastly, a calmer *Bacchanal* scene, dated to between 1959 and 1963, is set on a terrace or balcony shaded by vines. In one image three men sit listlessly whilst one plays a flute; this may be the aftermath of the second picture, from 1955, in which a naked mature man drinks wine to the sound of pipe and tambourine. In both scenes, though, naked younger males lean against the walls at either side, apparently awaiting something, although we may only speculate what that might be.

Closely comparable to Auguste Leveque's pictures are the bacchic works of Australian painter Norman Lindsay (1879–

112 Picasso may have been influenced to some degree by Jean Metzinger's *La danse, Bacchante* of 1906, a 'proto-Cubist' or Divisionist nude.

1969). There are strong pagan and erotic elements in his art, to the extent that he was called anti-Christian and decadent during his life time and had a large number of his paintings destroyed as pornographic by the US authorities. The artist's tastes are, perhaps, reflected by his decision to illustrate Petronius' *Satyricon* and his son Jack's *Dionysos: Nietzsche Contra Nietzsche. An Essay in Lyrical Philosophy* (1928).

Lindsay painted several pictures directly featuring Dionysos. The first of these was *Dionysus,* of 1908, in which the god stands on top of a small hill, surrounded by a seething mass of bodies-satyrs, leopards and Lindsay's trademark large breasted women. The god bears his thyrsos and is naked except for a loosely draped leopard skin. A naked maenad clings to him, others writhe, open mouthed and wild eyed, on all sides. It is noticeable that these are mature women, with heavy bosoms and round bellies.

The illustration, *Te Laudate, O Dionysus!* (I praise you, Dionysos), published in 1918, shows a curious procession of rejoicing people, of all ages and eras, clothed and unclothed, emerging from a wood. Thyrsoi are held aloft, Silenus is astride his donkey and satyrs prance. Lindsay twice tackled the story of Ariadne. An undated 'Study after Titian' shows a group of male and female bacchantes marching determinedly towards their destination, a small dog in tow (as in *Te Laudate).* The picture that seems to have been developed from this, *Bacchus and Ariadne* (1914), features yet another troop of fauns, leopards and naked men and women, but with Ariadne being carried on several men's shoulders.

Entourage (1940) is a less specific bacchanalian scene. Silenus, centaurs and fauns are present and naked women ride leopards, lions, gryphons and a deer. There's a lot of kissing and sexual touching. This is just one of a large number of such pictures that Lindsay created throughout his career, in which drunken men and women stagger, stumble and fall, satyrs cavort and centaurs prance. Sometimes there is evidence of wine drinking, sometimes we see bacchic elements such as pipes, tympana and leopard skins. Occasionally, live leopards are present, perhaps being ridden by naked teenage girls. It's not always clear what's happening, except that the participants are in a delirium of pleasure and sex is probably not very far away – the indication frequently being that the maenads will be pairing up.[113] With his crazed looking bacchantes, voluptuous nakedness and debauched behaviour, Lindsay's work epitomises the consensus on the bacchic rites that seems to have emerged over the last century and a half. He depicted riotous pleasure, with everything on the point of collapse – whether into bed or into a stupor.

Finally, I turn to an image from 1886 that truly encapsulates much of the spirit of these many images. In that year Austrian painter Gustav Klimt painted a memorable image of the *Altar of Dionysus* for a staircase in the newly completed *Burgtheater* in Vienna. Klimt often drew on Greek imagery to create aesthetic, mysterious and unsettlingly erotic pictures and the *Burgtheater* panel is no exception. In the painting, two naked adolescent girls, whom we may identify as maenads, appear before the god's shrine. One reclines, seemingly exhausted by the orgy, and languidly holds up some flowers whilst gazing straight out at the observer. The other girl presents a statue to the god; in contrast to her exhausted companion, she is a perfect creature who might almost have been carved from marble herself. She has immaculate pale, smooth skin, pert conical breasts, beautifully sculpted hair and darkly made-up eyes. To one side, a satyr figure plays on a drum and in the background lurk two young children with strangely black eyes – we may assume that their pupils have been hugely expanded by drugs.

Even today, in the twenty-first century, the taste for Bacchic art has far from abated. Examples include US artist Leonardo

113 These pictures include *Bacchanalia* (1923), *The Revellers* (1942), *Silenus Finds a Companion* (1940), *Scirocco, In the Wood, Procession, Bacchanal, or Village Festival* (1905), *Bacchanalian Revels* (1940), *Bacchanalian Scene* (1941), *Bacchanalian Festival* (1945) and *Bacchanalian Procession.*

Montoya, who has painted a huge pastoral bacchanal. It's a pastiche of images, with Bouguereau's *Bacchanal* forming the right-hand side of the canvas, his *Nymphaeum* the centre and his *Nymphs and Satyr* the left-hand half, to which are added some seated satyrs and an Aphrodite figure reminiscent of Walter Crane's *Renaissance of Venus*. The whole is a homage to the continuing power of these images. Polish painter Tomas Rut has followed in the tradition of Siemradski and Kotarbinski with his erotic, writhing *Bacchanal* dancers. Another young Polish painter, Paula Taranek, has created a portrait of Bacchus- a flower wreathed, if rather melancholy and middle-aged, vision of the god. *Bacchante* by Félix Hemme is a young woman caught in the act of stripping off her t-shirt and Valery Budanov's bacchantes are, likewise, essentially well-endowed glamour models. In 2012 contemporary British artist, Peregrine Roskilly, painted *The Triumph of Bacchus and Ariadne in Covent Garden.* Naked mythological figures borrowed from Titian and Carracci are updated and translated into central London, cycling through Covent Garden Plaza during a busy weekend. It's a joyous romp, with the god's leopards being reduced to a tabby cat riding on the rickshaw bearing the happy couple.[114]

CONCLUSION

At the start of this section, I queried whether the dismissal of all nineteenth century maenads as "simpering chorus girls" was accurate. I think the evidence contradicts this description. During the Victorian period the focus of artistic interest fell upon the female participant in the Dionysian rites, and this was primarily and precisely because they were sensuous, wild women, inspired by the god. It is notable at the same time how the Renaissance preference for group scenes of bacchanals was replaced by a

114 See the Saatchi Gallery for these artists' work.

preference for these single figures. A more personal interaction with the bacchantes was being suggested.

Simultaneously of course, this concentration on the devotee was at the expense of the god. Very few artists at all portrayed Dionysos-Bacchus. John Weguelin was a very rare exception. His *Bacchus Triumphant* of 1882 renders the god as a jolly young boy, being carried astride a large wine jar in a procession, brandishing a thyrsos. *Bacchus and the Choir of Nymphs* (1888) imagines the deity as a handsome young man, reclining languidly on a leopard skin. However, he is outnumbered by half a dozen semi-naked nymphs, drawing our attention back once again to the female entourage and their sexuality rather than the divinity and his powers.

Modern Rites

> "Blessed is he who, being fortunate and knowing the rites of the gods, keeps his life pure and has his soul initiated into the Bacchic revels, dancing in inspired frenzy over the mountains with holy purifications, and who, revering the mysteries of great mother Kybele, brandishing the thyrsos, garlanded with ivy, serves Dionysos."[115]

Modern pagan and polytheist groups often include worship of Dionysos in their traditions and practices, most prominently those which have sought to revive ancient Hellenic polytheism, such as the Supreme Council of Ethnic Hellenes.

The practitioners of the reconstructed religion of classical Greece seek to restore traditional festivals of the gods. They collate information on rites and ceremonies from a range of primary and secondary sources so that they can revive the original practices as accurately as possible. Reciting hymns to Dionysos, especially the Orphic hymns, is a key element common to all festivals honouring the god. In addition, libations of wine are offered, as are grape vines, ivy, and various forms of incense, particularly styrax.

The Lenaia festival is celebrated by drinking, merriment and the performance of plays, especially Aristophanes' *The Frogs*. The Anthesteria is celebrated by drinking watered-down wine and making garlands to celebrate the coming of spring. Honouring the dead also remains important. Some celebrants offer the dead a meal: 'panspermia,' a soup of mixed beans and wheat grain, is considered to be the most appropriate dish, but eggs, leeks and garlic are also suitable.

Interested readers may note that there are several of these Hellenic pagan organisations in existence, in North America as

115 Euripides, *Bacchae*, 73–80.

well as in Europe, and there is plentiful information available online about them and the revived rites. At the same time, though, it's worth recording what was said in Part One about the ancient cult of Dionysos. There was no single, 'official' creed and different practices were followed at different places across the classical world, from Asia Minor to Iberia. Scholars have therefore preferred to speak of the ancient *cults* of Dionysos. Individuals are free, therefore, to develop whatever principles and practices feel best for them.

Conclusions

"Ecstasy's the birth-right of our gang..."[116]

Dionysos is the god of epiphany. He has been called the 'coming god' – the one who enters people's lives and peoples' personalities. He is, too, the god who is coming to join the party – he's about to manifest himself in the fumes of wine and dope.

Another aspect of this changeable and impending nature may be the fact that Dionysos' cult is constantly evolving: as one authority summarised it, "outburst and revolution belong to the very essence of the god." Views of the god changed over antiquity and they continue to develop even in the twenty-first century.[117]

Dionysos is also a private and individual god. The Dionysian mysteries developed outside any system of state sponsored religion; they were private celebrations and featured individual initiations. There was no need for a formal priesthood or hierarchy; the rites were, fundamentally, personal and communal revelations. This means he is directly accessible to each of us; we may each contact him and enter into our own dialogue.

Over the course of the centuries in classical times, the nature of the cult of Dionysos evolved. There was a shift away from blood sacrifice, most especially of humans, and the religious movement became generally less assertive and evangelical. It seems that it needed to be aggressive to establish itself, but that then the focus of attention turned inward. This is reflected particularly well by the changes in the nature of the maenads. The stories of their earliest exploits depict them fighting and destroying the god's enemies. Later, they became spiritual amazons; their frenzy

116 From 'The Whole Shebang,' song by Maxwell Demon in the film *Velvet Goldmine*, 1998.

117 Burkert, *Greek Religion*, 290.

was directed not against opponents but against obstacles within themselves that stood in the way of union with the god.

Those maenads, in particular, are what continue to fascinate us. Their energy and independence, their single-minded devotion to the god that carries them outside the bounds of conventional conduct, are inspiring and attractive. Their courage to connect directly with the deity offers a model for a different way of experiencing the divine and gives a new meaning to ecstasy. The modern approach to Dionysos is through a practical mysticism. It is not about doctrines, philosophy or symbolism, but rather involves a direct interaction with the ineffable or transcendental.

Lightning Source UK Ltd.
Milton Keynes UK
UKHW021322070422
401221UK00008B/208